FORENSIC ANTHROPOLOGY

SCIENCE & TECHNOLOGY IN FOCUS

FORENSIC ANTHROPOLOGY

The Growing Science of Talking Bones

Peggy Thomas

Facts On File, Inc.

This book is dedicated to my father

HOWARD FACKLAM.

As a teacher he taught me to look at the world and its facts,
but as my father he showed me the world and its graces.

Thanks Dad!

Facts On File, Inc.
132 West 31st Street
New York NY 10001

Library of Congress Cataloging-in-Publication Data

Thomas, Peggy.
Forensic anthropology : the growing science of talking bones / Peggy Thomas.
p. cm. — (Science and technology in focus)
Rev. ed. of: Talking bones. c1995.
Includes bibliographical references and index.
ISBN 0-8160-4731-6 (hardcover)
1. Forensic anthropology. 2. Forensic osteology. I. Thomas, Peggy.
Talking bones. II. Title. III. Series.
GN69.8 .T48 2003
599.9—dc21   2002005703

Facts On File books are available at special discounts when purchased in bulk quantities for
businesses, associations, institutions, or sales promotions. Please call our Special Sales
Department in New York at (212) 967-8800 or (800) 322-8755.

You can find Facts On File on the World Wide Web at http://www.factsonfile.com

Text design by Erika K. Arroyo
Cover design by Nora Wertz
Illustrations by Sholto Ainslie, Patricia Meschino, and
Dale Williams © Facts On File, Inc.

Printed in the United States of America

MP FOF 10 9 8 7 6 5 4 3

This book is printed on acid-free paper.

CONTENTS

ACKNOWLEDGMENTS

I would like to thank all the people who shared their expertise and anecdotes with me, especially those who worked tirelessly sifting through rubble to recover the remains of those lost on September 11, 2001. Thank you to Frank Saul, regional commander of DMORT V; Julie Mather Saul, director of the Forensic Anthropology Lab at the Lucas County Coroner's Office; and Dennis Dirkmaat of Mercyhurst College. I extend my thanks to Kevin Smith at the Buffalo Museum of Science for teaching me about Nes-min, and to my family for surviving yet another whirlwind round of writing frenzy. As always, I appreciate the help and advice of Fran Thomas, as well as Margery and Howard Facklam, who read early drafts and helped with research, Lisa Kirch for photo research, and Frank K. Darmstadt and Cynthia Yazbek for their editorial direction.

INTRODUCTION

The science of forensic anthropology has grown tremendously since *Talking Bones* was first published.

This new edition updates the reader on the most current research being conducted—everything from the biochemical processes of decomposition to the newest techniques for identifying a person from the smallest bone fragments. It also describes the growing use of computer technology to record information, analyze statistics, and approximate faces from a skull.

Revised chapters examine the work of forensic anthropologists who uncover evidence of human rights abuse in war-ravaged countries and bring our military's missing in action home to rest. Several new chapters also explore related fields of study including DNA profiling, forensic dentistry, and forensic entomology, the study of insects at a crime scene.

Each section details real forensic cases, some of which come directly from news headlines: mass graves in Bosnia, the controversy over the ancient remains known as Kennewick Man, and the painstaking recovery and identification of victims of the September 11, 2001, World Trade Center terrorist attack.

HUMAN SKELETON

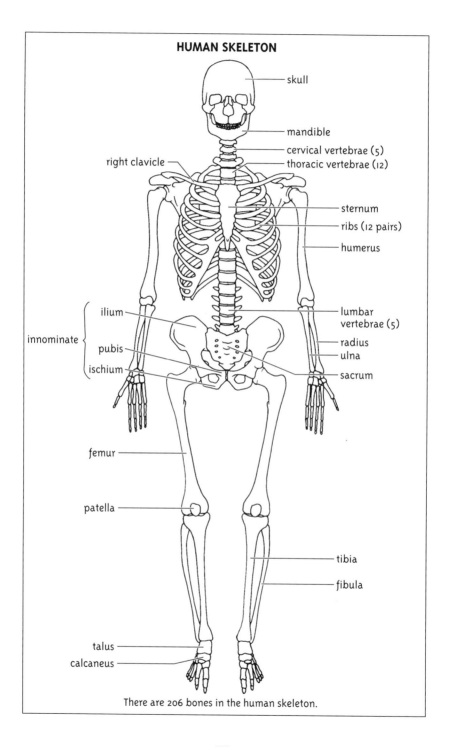

skull

mandible

cervical vertebrae (5)

thoracic vertebrae (12)

right clavicle

sternum

ribs (12 pairs)

humerus

lumbar vertebrae (5)

ilium

radius

innominate

pubis

ulna

ischium

sacrum

femur

patella

tibia

fibula

talus

calcaneus

There are 206 bones in the human skeleton.

HUMAN SKULL—FRONT AND SIDE VIEWS

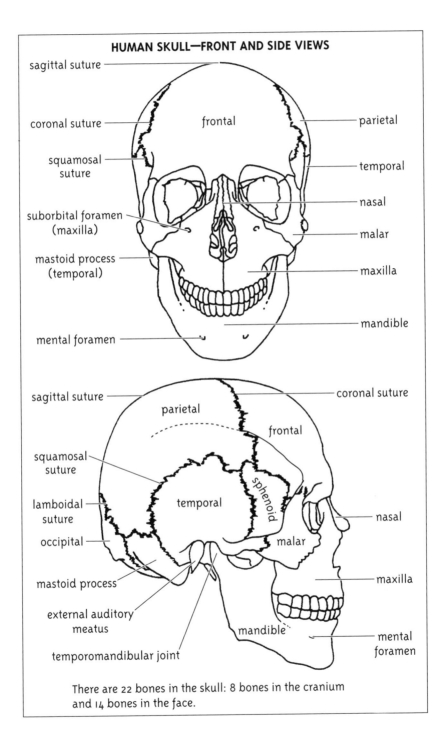

sagittal suture

coronal suture

squamosal suture

suborbital foramen (maxilla)

mastoid process (temporal)

mental foramen

frontal

parietal

temporal

nasal

malar

maxilla

mandible

sagittal suture

squamosal suture

lamboidal suture

occipital

mastoid process

external auditory meatus

temporomandibular joint

parietal

frontal

sphenoid

temporal

malar

coronal suture

nasal

maxilla

mandible

mental foramen

There are 22 bones in the skull: 8 bones in the cranium and 14 bones in the face.

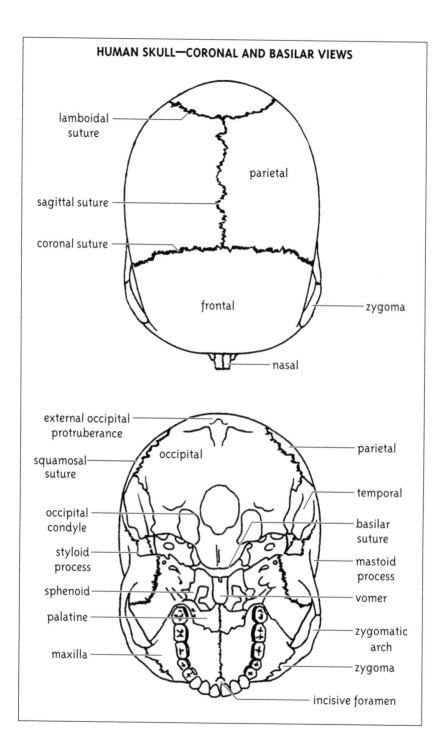

HUMAN SKULL—CORONAL AND BASILAR VIEWS

lamboidal suture

parietal

sagittal suture

coronal suture

frontal

zygoma

nasal

external occipital protruberance

parietal

occipital

squamosal suture

temporal

occipital condyle

basilar suture

styloid process

mastoid process

sphenoid

vomer

palatine

zygomatic arch

maxilla

zygoma

incisive foramen

MURDER

Within the archives of our skeletons are written down the intimate diaries of our lives: our ancestry, our illnesses, our injuries and infirmities, the patterns of our labor and exercise, sometimes even our most secret sins and blush worthy abuses . . . To read all of these things—that is the art of forensic anthropology.

—William Maples, former director of the C. A. Pound
Human Identification Laboratory

September 11, 2001

While this book was being written, a new chapter in U.S. history was being written as well. On September 11, 2001, two commercial airliners were hijacked by terrorists and flown into the twin towers of the World Trade Center in New York City. Another jet hit the Pentagon in Virginia, and a fourth plane crashed into a coalfield outside of Shanksville, Pennsylvania. Instantly, rescue crews and *forensic* specialists were called to the sites to do what they had trained long, hard hours to do, but even that was unheard of given the unbelievable and bizarre circumstances. And then, within two hours of the first attack, both of the World Trade Center towers collapsed and changed forensic investigations forever.

Never in the history of forensics had investigators been faced with a single crime scene so immense, violence so destructive, or a mass murder with so many victims. The debris from the two 110-story buildings covered more than 16 acres and was compressed into a pile of rubble nine stories high. The combined destruction of the crashed planes, the combustion of the full tanks of jet fuel, and the impact of more than two billion pounds of steel, glass, and concrete crashing to the ground would make the job of identifying all of the thousands of victims nearly impossible.

But the forensic anthropologist's job description is just that—nearly impossible. These professionals are supposed to examine the bones of the dead to determine the characteristics of someone's life. Was the person male or female, right-handed or left-handed, tall or short? Did

In an unprecedented rescue effort, hundreds of workers formed a bucket-brigade line to carefully remove the debris to uncover the thousands of people trapped underneath the collapsed World Trade Center towers. [FEMA]

the man suffer backaches? Had the woman given birth? These are the kinds of questions forensic anthropologists are trained to answer.

The destruction of September 11 created an unprecedented challenge, one that forensic anthropologists and other investigators took up without flinching. They pushed themselves and their science to answer the questions that were before them. In turn, their knowledge and technology will expand, because like all forensic sciences, forensic anthropology owes its very existence to crime. The more treacherous and devious murderers have become, the more knowledgeable forensic anthropologists have become. The science has grown in its use of technology, its expanse of knowledge of the human skeleton, the process of death, the effects of disease, aging, weapons, and fire. The best examples of detective work in the field are the direct result of some of the most heinous murders. A "who's who" list of the people who figure prominently in the history of forensic anthropology includes not only scientists but victims and killers as well. Barely 30 years old as a sanctioned branch of forensic science, forensic anthropology has come a long way from the seedy criminal cases that marked its beginning.

The Sausage Maker

Old man Luetgert made sausage from his wife.
He turned up the steam.
She began to scream.
There'll be a hot time in the old town tonight.

In 1897, along the streets of Chicago you could hear children skipping rope to this morbid refrain as the trial of Adolph Luetgert filled the front pages of the local newspapers.

Adolph Luetgert was a well-known sausage maker in Chicago, and when his wife, Louisa, mysteriously disappeared, he claimed that she had run off to relatives after an argument. But the neighbors became suspicious when Luetgert's two young sons began to ask door-to-door if anyone had seen their mother. Six days later, in order to stop the rumors, Luetgert finally reported Louisa's disappearance to the police.

Police Captain Herman Schuettler and a team of officers interviewed people in the neighborhood who described Luetgert as a wife beater and adulterer. Luetgert did not even live in the house with his family but slept in a back office of the five-story sausage factory on the corner of Diversey and Hermitage Streets. Business associates told police about Luetgert's ambitious attempts to increase his sausage-making business, even though his wife disapproved.

Schuettler suspected Luetgert of murder, but he needed evidence to prove it. Police questioned the workers in the sausage factory who informed them that weeks before the disappearance of his wife, Luetgert made an unusual order of 375 pounds of potash and 50 pounds of arsenic to be delivered to the factory.

The night guard told the police that on the night of his wife's disappearance Luetgert sent him on an errand and then gave him the rest of the night off. The guard left Luetgert in the sausage factory, stirring a boiling liquid in a huge cooking vat. The guard had never seen his employer do that before, and according to the other employees, Luetgert fired up the furnace under the vat and kept vigil all night. The next morning, employees found a greasy substance all over the floor beneath the vat, and Luetgert asleep in his office.

Witnesses claimed they saw Luetgert and his wife entering the factory late in the evening, and others swore they heard screams coming from inside the building. Schuettler ordered his men to search the factory—to look inside crates, under machinery, and inside the cooking vats. The vat Luetgert had personally kept boiling that infamous night was drained through a spigot at its base as officers sat around the foul-smelling sludge, poking through it with wooden sticks. And in the putrid slime they found the evidence—a small bone, a ring guard, and a wedding ring with the engraving *L.L.* on the inside. A further search of the ashes outside the building uncovered a bone hairpin, a steel corset stay, several bone fragments, and a false tooth.

Experts from the University of Chicago reported to the police that boiling potash and arsenic would have dissolved a human body within two hours. The potash would have leached out most of the calcium from Louisa's bones—reducing them to a jelly (the greasy substance noticed on the floor). Based on all this evidence, Luetgert was arrested for the murder of his wife.

Adolph may have cooked his wife, but the rumor spread that he made sausage from her too. The more the children sang, the faster sausage sales dropped in the Chicago area.

Charles Deneen, the Illinois State's attorney was assigned to prosecute at the trial, but he had a problem. How could he prove a murder actually took place without having a body to prove it? At the trial, Deneen called Luetgert "one of the most dastardly murderers in history," "an inhuman fiend" who sat and watched his wife sink into the boiling vat, but Luetgert's defense attorney produced witnesses who

George Dorsey was the first anthropologist to testify in court regarding the identity of bones found at a crime scene.
[The Field Museum, Neg. # A108072]

claimed they saw Louisa at a railroad station 50 miles away. The jury was confused and deadlocked. The judge dismissed them and called for another jury.

A second trial was prepared with a new jury, but the prosecutor was still having difficulty proving murder. To Deneen's dismay, Dr. Walter H. Allport of the Chicago Medical College, who was called to testify, declared that the remains "may be human, but just as likely they may be from some lower animal."

Needing real expertise to win this case, Prosecutor Deneen called on George Dorsey, a curator of physical anthropology at the Field Museum of Natural History in Chicago, whose specialty was the study of ancient human remains. Dorsey had spent his career researching how to determine sex from a skeleton. This case was right up his alley.

After examining the bone fragments, Dorsey testified, "I have found no bones from the hog, dog, or sheep which have any of the characteristics which distinguish these bones. In my judgment, they belong to one human body." In total, the four bones were so small they would have fit on a tablespoon. They included the end of a metacarpal from the hand, a head of a rib, and a portion of a phalanx, or toe bone.

Dorsey testified that the small bone found in the vat was the sesamoid bone from the joint of the big toe. The sesamoid, named because it resembles a sesame seed, is embedded in the tendons of the toe and acts as a ball bearing that helps the human foot to bend.

A columnist for the *Chicago Tribune* observed Dorsey in the courtroom and was impressed with what he saw. "His knowledge was so well systematized, so well in hand, so sound, precise and broad, that it was a pleasure to listen to him: it is not often one comes in contact with a brain of so fine a fiber, so vigorous, and so sane."

Dorsey's testimony bolstered the already damaging evidence against Luetgert, and the case was closed. Luetgert was convicted and sentenced to life in prison.

The Luetgert trial was the first time an anthropologist took the witness stand in a forensic case in the United States. It was clear that a physical anthropologist, someone who studies the human body and how groups of humans differ physically, might know more about human bones than a medical doctor. Unfortunately, Dorsey discovered the difficulties of breaking into forensic work. His academic career suffered when colleagues complained that he had "lowered" himself by "performing" at a trial, and others could not believe that he had the nerve to challenge the testimony of a medical doctor. Because of this, Dorsey dropped his forensic pursuits and devoted himself to photography and the study of Native Americans.

But Dorsey's testimony opened the door for other anthropologists who, until then, had only consulted for law enforcement quietly in their labs. The methodology Dorsey used to determine that the bones in the vat were the remains of Louisa Luetgert had already been established in court only a short time before in another grisly murder trial.

The Parkman Murder

The Friday before Thanksgiving, 1849, Dr. George Parkman walked through Boston, Massachusetts, as he did every day, running errands and visiting patients. He was a prominent physician and a wealthy man noted for his land dealings. On this particular Friday, he was on his way to the Parkman Medical Building at the Harvard Medical School, named after him because he had donated the land on which it was built.

On the way, Parkman stopped to buy a head of lettuce from the local grocer, leaving it there to be picked up when he returned. At the

$3,000 REWARD!

DR. GEORGE PARKMAN,

A well known citizen of Boston, left his residence
No. 8 Walnut Street, on Friday last, he is 60 years of age ;—about 5 feet 9 inches high—grey hair—thin face— with a scar under his chin—light complexion—and usually walks very fast. He was dressed in a dark frock coat, dark pantaloons, purple silk vest, with dark figured black stock and black hat.

As he may have wandered from home in consequence of some sudden aberration of mind, being perfectly well when he left his house; or, as he had with him a large sum of money, he may have been foully dealt with. The above reward will be paid for information which will lead to his discovery if alive; or for the detection and conviction of the perpetrators if any injury may have been done to him.

A suitable reward will be paid for the discovery of his body.

Boston, Nov. 26th, 1849.   **ROBERT G. SHAW.**

Information may be given to the City Marshal.

From the Congress Printing House,(Farwell & Co.) 32 Congress St.

Twenty-eight thousand handbills were posted throughout Boston in an attempt to get information about Parkman's whereabouts. [Courtesy of the Massachusetts Historical Society]

medical school, Parkman met with another prominent physician and professor, Dr. John Webster, who was noted for enjoying life. An avid gambler, Webster had borrowed heavily from Parkman to cover debts, and it was this debt that Parkman was coming to collect. According to Webster, he and Parkman had a pleasant conversation, and he paid his debt willingly. After Parkman received the money, he left and Webster claimed he never saw him again.

But Parkman never picked up the lettuce, and he never returned home. His brother-in-law called the police and later posted 28,000 handbills across the city offering a $3,000 reward for information of Parkman's whereabouts.

The police questioned the amiable Webster about his meeting with Parkman and took his statement, but they did not suspect Webster of murder. In fact, they were not convinced there had been any foul play at all.

On the other hand, Ephraim Littlefield, the janitor at the medical school, was very suspicious. He claimed that Webster had been acting unusually kind, giving Littlefield the week off, and sending a Thanksgiving turkey to his home.

Littlefield roamed every inch of the medical building he knew so well, looking for evidence. He found nothing until he went into the basement, which was made up of several chambers, or pits, that collected sewage and debris from the rooms above. These pits then emptied into the river, which carried the foul smells and gunk away.

As Littlefield later told the jury, on a hunch he went to the stone pit that sat underneath Webster's office and latrine. With his wife holding a lantern above him, Littlefield used a pickax to break through the stone wall. In the dim light he peered in, and there he saw a hacked-up body hanging on a hook similar to the ones used to hold cadavers in the medical school upstairs. In the dirt and slime at the bottom of the pit, he found the remains of a pelvis.

The police found the rest. Searching through Webster's office, they discovered the rib section in a tea chest and a set of false teeth in the oven. They also found body parts in the anatomy lab, where they might have otherwise gone unnoticed, and burned bone and a button in the furnace. It appeared that Parkman was all over the place. Webster was arrested that evening and taken to jail.

A team of doctors from the Harvard Medical College was called in to examine and identify the remains. The team included Jefferies Wyman, an anatomist at the college; a dentist, Nathan Keep; and Oliver Wendell Holmes, dean of the Medical College, an anatomist (and father of the younger Oliver Wendell Holmes who would grow up to be a justice on the United States Supreme Court).

First, the team toured the scene of the crime, inspecting where the remains were found. Then, the 150-odd bones collected from the medical building were laid out and examined. It was Wyman's job to reassemble them in anatomical order. He determined that those parts found in the lab were not proper lab specimens because they had not been treated with preserving chemicals. The team agreed that they were indeed human remains because of the shape of the pelvis and teeth. They proceeded to identify the remains as those from a male 50 to 60 years old and 5 feet 10 inches tall. Parkman was 60 years old when he died and had stood 5 feet 11 inches.

Nathan Keep was on the team because he was Parkman's dentist. Parkman had ordered a new set of dentures to wear at the groundbreaking ceremony of the medical building and told Keep he would not pay if they were not ready in time. Keep managed to finish Parkman's new set of false teeth in time by using a mold of Parkman's unusually prominent jutting jaw, which had earned Parkman the nickname "Chin."

Dr. Keep examined the charred and battered false teeth and testified that this set, which was found in Webster's oven, was the same set he had made for Parkman. He showed the jurors the unusual shape of the denture plate that would fit only Parkman.

When the trial opened on March 19, 1850, it was the biggest show in town, with the bones as the star witness. With the help of the doctors and the dentist, the prosecutor was able to convince the jury to bring in a guilty verdict, and Webster was sentenced to hang.

More than a century later, historians have raised questions about Webster's guilt, based on the mishandling of the trial. Some researchers have questioned whether the remains truly were Parkman's or whether they were planted by an unscrupulous Littlefield to get the $3,000 reward. We may never know.

Nevertheless, the Webster trial set the standard procedure for analyzing bones that every forensic anthropologist uses today, which must answer a series of ten questions:

1. Are the bones human?
2. How many individuals are represented?
3. How long ago did death occur?
4. What was the person's age at death?
5. What was the person's sex?
6. What was the person's race?
7. What was the person's height?
8. Are there any identifying characteristics, such as old injuries, disease, or unusual features (such as Parkman's chin)?
9. What was the cause of death?
10. What was the manner of death (homicide, suicide, accidental, natural, or unknown)?

The trials of Webster and Luetgert were sensational in their day, but they were also the exceptions to an unspoken rule of the early 19th century. Professors did not venture far, or for too long, into the courts. Police work was still viewed as an art, the application of subjective intuition and cunning to solve a puzzle. Although scientists were occasionally consulted, it was not the norm. But attitudes would soon change. Crime rates rose in London and Paris and other burgeoning European cities, and the need for alternative investigating methods grew. Law enforcement was desperate to find ways to keep track of career criminals, at the same time when scientists were seeking answers to questions of criminal behavior, causes of death, and identity.

BUILDING A SCIENCE

For physical (and forensic) anthropologists, bodies equal data.

—Christopher Joyce and Eric Stover, *Witnesses from the Grave*, 1991

In the late 1800s, science and the art of detection were on a collision course. Scientists eagerly proposed social theories and then devised scientific means of proving them, while metropolitan police investigators were struggling to keep abreast of the criminal mind. There had to be a better way to identify and catch criminals. Scientists studied convicts and patients in asylums, analyzed their behavior as well as their physical features, and using a common practice called *anthropometry*, the systematic measurement of the human body, some scientists developed a primitive form of criminal profiling.

Franz Josef Gall, in 1796, developed the field of phrenology, the study of bumps on a person's head. He proposed that cranial topography revealed a person's behavioral tendencies. If someone had bumps on the forehead they were highly intelligent. Bumps on the top of the head were a sign of morality, and bumps on the sides of the head just above the ears indicated selfishness. Phrenology became a popular theory in the 19th century and proponents claimed to be able to measure a person's head to diagnose stinginess, drunkenness, and 40 other characteristics.

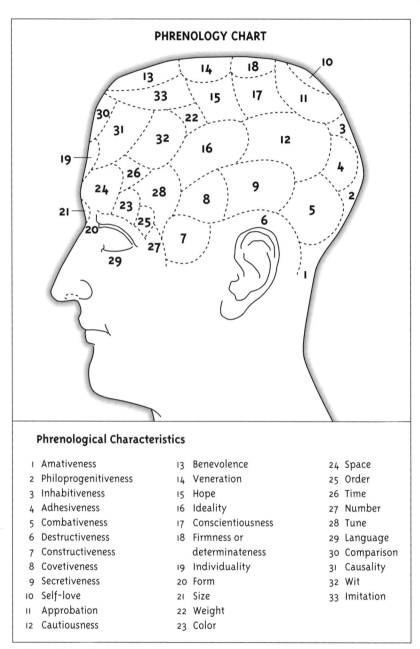

PHRENOLOGY CHART

Phrenological Characteristics

1 Amativeness	13 Benevolence	24 Space
2 Philoprogenitiveness	14 Veneration	25 Order
3 Inhabitiveness	15 Hope	26 Time
4 Adhesiveness	16 Ideality	27 Number
5 Combativeness	17 Conscientiousness	28 Tune
6 Destructiveness	18 Firmness or	29 Language
7 Constructiveness	determinateness	30 Comparison
8 Covetiveness	19 Individuality	31 Causality
9 Secretiveness	20 Form	32 Wit
10 Self-love	21 Size	33 Imitation
11 Approbation	22 Weight	
12 Cautiousness	23 Color	

Before anthropologists measured bones to identify the dead, phrenologists measured and mapped the human skull to diagnose more than 30 different physical and social characteristics.

In 1876, Cesare Lombroso, a medical superintendent of a lunatic asylum in Pesaro, Italy, published a paper, "L'uomo Delinquente," on the physical traits of the criminal man. He saw anatomy as destiny. Lombroso explained how his study of more than 6,000 convicts revealed that there were specific physical traits that could be used to identify a born delinquent. He described the criminal type as having a thick skull, high cheekbones, a heavy brow, large handle-shaped ears, a wide jaw, long arms, large deep-set eyes, and a narrow field of vision. He further described "fire raisers," or arsonists, as having small heads. Swindlers had unusually heavy builds, and pickpockets were tall, dark-haired, and had long hands. He inferred that the crudest members of society (usually the poor) had evolved little from other animal branches of the evolutionary tree. At the 4th International Congress on Criminal Anthropology, Lombroso suggested that the outlines of prostitutes' feet looked prehensile like that of monkeys.

These ideas worked their way into European courtrooms where Lombroso testified as an expert witness. No matter how law-abiding a man was, if he fit the description, he could be mistaken for a criminal and hanged. In *Crime: Its Causes and Remedies* (1911) Lombroso recalled one trial he testified in and said:

> Upon examination I found that this man had outstanding ears, great maxillaries [jaw bones] and cheekbones . . . division of the frontal bone, premature wrinkles, sinister look, nose twisted to the right—in short, a physiognomy approaching the criminal type . . . joined with the other evidence, [his physical description] would have been enough to convict him in a country less tender toward criminals.

Fortunately, in this instance, the man was acquitted.

A number of instruments were developed to measure these criminal tendencies. A craniometer traced the shape of a suspect's head onto paper, and a ball on a string was swung like a pendulum in front of a person's face to measure his field of vision. But no real evidence ever materialized to connect physical appearance and criminal behavior.

The Measure of Man

Alphonse Bertillon (1853–1914), a French clerk who worked for the Prefecture of Police in Paris, proposed one method of anthropometry that did take hold for at least a short time. In his lifetime he managed to change the process of criminology. Bertillon, a son of a physician and anthropologist, was expelled from every school he attended. Academic interests did not hold his attention, but the work of his father and grandfather did. They measured everyone who visited their house in an attempt to prove a theory hypothesized by a Belgian astronomer and statistician, Adolphe Quetelet, that no two persons had identical physical measurements. During Bertillon's tenure as a police clerk, he transcribed police officers' vague descriptions of arrested men and women and filed badly processed photographs, all the while thinking there must be a better way of identifying recidivists, or repeat offenders. After only eight months on the job, Bertillon devised a system based on the criminal's physical measurements.

Bertillon appealed to the prefect of police several times before finally, in 1882, being granted time and space to experiment with his identification system. The prefect gave Bertillon three months and the use of two clerks to prove that his idea would work. With calipers and measuring tape, he and his assistants measured more than 1,800 criminals in that time period. For every criminal, Bertillon recorded a list of 11 measurements: the length, breadth, and diameter of the head, length of the left forearm, width of outstretched arms, height sitting, height standing, length of left middle and little fingers, length of the left foot and length of the right ear, as well as gait (the way someone walks), eye color, and dress. It was called a *portrait parle*, a spoken picture.

His criminal identification system was based on three assumptions: that the dimensions of the bones in an adult skeleton did not change over time; the mathematical probability of two adults sharing the same measurements for two of the 11 measurements was 16 to 1; and the chance that two adults shared all 11 measurements was 4,191,304 to 1. Knowing all this, Bertillon was confident that he could determine whether a criminal had been arrested before, even when he or she used an alias.

Just two weeks before the end of the trial period, Bertillon recorded the measurements of a man named Dupont. The name meant nothing because it was common for repeat offenders to use several aliases. The name Dupont was popular—it was the sixth Dupont he had measured that day. But the face was familiar, and Bertillon had a feeling that he had measured this person before. He searched his index cards until he came up with a file that had the same measurements as those of Dupont, although the name on the card was Martin. Confronted with the evidence, the man confessed his true identity. The French police were delighted that Bertillon's system worked. More successes followed, and soon the French police adopted Bertillonage as their primary identification system.

Bertillon received much notoriety and a promotion. He became the director of the Judicial Identification Service. By 1888, Bertillon had an archive of nearly half a million *portraits parle*. The success in France prompted other countries, including the United States, to set up their own Bertillonage files.

As successful as the system seemed, it was cumbersome, complex, and prone to errors. The measurements had to be exact, and there were many codes and formulas to memorize. It was too difficult for the average police clerk to master. Experiments with another identification system, called dactylography, or fingerprinting, threatened Bertillonage and ultimately replaced it.

The U.S. prison system adopted Bertillonage in 1887 so that every prisoner entering the system was measured and photographed. But one case in 1903 clearly showed the fatal flaw in the system. It involved two prisoners at the federal prison in Leavenworth, Kansas. On May 1, Will West was sent to the Bertillonage officer to be measured. The clerk thought he looked familiar, but West denied ever being in prison before. When the clerk filed the card away, he came across the file of a William West. The two men were brought together. They still denied they were related, although later it was discovered that they each wrote to the same brother, the same uncle, and the same five sisters. Under the Bertillonage system the identification cards of two men were the same. Bertillonage did not take into account identical twin criminals. The feature that clearly identified the two Wests as individuals were the men's fingerprints. That one case convinced authorities to drop Bertillonage and replace it with fingerprinting.

A Turning Point

Although measuring bodies was no longer being done in police stations and prisons, it was still carried out in university laboratories. While Bertillon was measuring criminals in France, anatomist Thomas Dwight (1843–1911) was measuring cadavers at Harvard University in Boston. Although he did take part in a few legal cases, none were remarkable or written about. His contribution to forensics took place in the classroom, not the courtroom. Some people in the field believe Dwight earned the title of "father of forensic anthropology" because he set a new course for himself and his students. He diverged from the norm of anatomy and moved bone analysis toward anthropology—toward the study of groups of humans and what distinguishes them physically from one another.

Like Bertillon, Dwight also believed that the bones of the human body reflected the various traits of the individual. He was successful in proving that a bone expert could measure a single bone and accurately "read" various conclusions from it about a person's height, sex, and age and write an "osteobiography," a skeletal history of that person's life. His landmark essay on the subject, "The Identification of the Human Skeleton: A Medico Legal Study," was published in 1878. Dwight went on to devise a way to calculate a skeleton's height from the measurement of the sternum, or breastbone, and show that a person's sex could be deciphered from looking at the articular surfaces, or ends, of the long bones in the legs and arms.

Once Dwight set the course, it was up to his students like George Dorsey to take the techniques he and his colleagues developed and apply them to courtroom cases like the Luetgert trial. But it would take many more murders and monographs to make forensic anthropology an official forensic science. That did not happen for 100 years, when in 1973 the American Academy of Forensic Sciences created a new division for physical anthropology. There were 14 members that first year, and the following year they outlined the procedures for accreditation. Today, there are more than 200 members in the academy, some of whom have been working with law enforcement agencies like the Federal Bureau of Investigation for many years.

Partners in Crime Fighting

The National Museum of Natural History at the Smithsonian Institution in Washington, D.C., has one of the finest anthropology departments in the country. Its long hallways on the fifth floor are lined with floor-to-ceiling cupboards filled with more than 33,000 skeletons that make up one of the largest human skeletal reference collections in the world. Until the 1930s, this collection was used only for academic purposes, but then the Smithsonian got a new neighbor.

The Federal Bureau of Investigation (FBI) moved into the J. Edgar Hoover Building down the street, and like all good neighbors, they helped each other. In 1936, the curator of physical anthropology at the Smithsonian, Ales Hrdlicka, came to the attention of the FBI when he gave testimony before a committee of the House of Representatives.

The Smithsonian
Institution's
33,000 skeletons
housed in these
cabinets comprise
one of the largest
skeletal collections
in the world.
(©Chip Clark/
NMNH, Smithsonian
Institution)

FBI officials at the time described him as "the best informed man in the United States on anthropology." Two years later, J. Edgar Hoover, the director of the FBI, asked for Hrdlicka's help in analyzing human remains. FBI agents would lug body parts over to the museum to be examined by Hrdlicka, and over a 40-year career, he consulted on at least 37 cases.

Although he had a lengthy relationship with the FBI, filling countless files within the bureau, Hrdlicka never presented or published any of his findings. There was still a stigma attached to forensic work, an internal battle between purely academic and applied sciences. Even though anthropologists examined bones for the police now and then, it was never considered appropriate behavior, and certainly not the foundation for a career as it now is becoming. Forensics was seldom discussed or written about.

But the 1930s was the era of gangsters, and the activities of criminals like Al Capone and Machine Gun Kelly kept the FBI in business and the Smithsonian in bodies. Perhaps it was because of these cases that the bureau seemed more interested in promoting forensic anthropology than academic institutions were. In 1939, the FBI published the landmark paper that effectively let forensic anthropology out of the closet. It appeared in the *FBI Law Enforcement Bulletin* and was called "Guide to the Identification of Human Skeletal Material" by Wilton Marion Krogman. It highlighted the potential contributions that forensic anthropology could make to society and suggested that forensic work was a legitimate and necessary application of the science.

Other law enforcement agencies began to contact anthropologists more readily when a skeletonized body was discovered, and FBI agents were calling on the curator of anthropology at the Smithsonian more frequently. When Hrdlicka retired in 1942, his successor, Dale Stewart, formalized the relationship between the bureau and the Smithsonian and went on to train two generations of scientists and FBI agents. In 1979, he wrote the first textbook for forensic anthropologists, and

Anthropologists at the Smithsonian examine skeletal remains for the FBI and other law enforcement agencies around the country. [©Chip Clark/NMNH, Smithsonian Institution]

during his tenure with the FBI he consulted on 167 cases. In 1962, J. Lawrence Angel took over Stewart's position, and during a 15-year period, he reported on 646 legal cases.

Today, Douglas Ubelaker and Douglas Owsley, both curators of physical anthropology at the Smithsonian, consult for the FBI. Like their predecessors, Ubelaker and Owsley divide their time between the 40 or so forensic cases that are sent over from the FBI each year and their academic research on the Meso-American Indians and prehistoric and pioneer remains of the Great Plains, respectively.

Any evidence brought to the FBI is handled by the FBI's Evidence Control Center, which assigns and distributes the evidence to the proper division for analysis. Fingerprint evidence is sent to the Identification Division, bloodstained articles to the Serology Lab, and spent bullets to Ballistics. Some material such as ransom notes may need to be sent to more than one lab for examination, and it is the Control Center's job to prioritize the proper sequence, because some lab tests alter the evidence. Chemical processing for fingerprints, for example, may ruin potential evidence from a bloodstain on a ransom note.

All human skeletal remains are first sent to the FBI's Hair and Fiber Unit. From there, special agents send it on to the museum. Together they have identified bodies that come to the FBI from all over the country. If odd bones are picked up by someone walking through the woods, for example (and this does happen, as Ubelaker explains), Ubelaker can tell whether the remains are human or animal. Most of the cases that arrive are marked with a *Q*, which stands for questioned material. The FBI may have some idea or a strong suspicion as to the identity of the remains, but they are presented to Ubelaker as unknown. This preserves the examiner's objectivity and eliminates the possibility that other people's judgments could influence the results. The Smithsonian's anthropology department also aids the FBI by creating clay reconstructions of a person's face, superimposing portraits with skulls, and conducting microscopic analysis.

War and Research

A science is only as credible as its research, and anthropologists who had given testimony in the witness chair knew that credibility could only come with a broader database, more exact procedures, and unshakable statistics. But it is hard to do research in forensic anthropology because you need human bodies to study, and lots of them.

Before the 1940s, most of the information about sex, ethnicity, age, and stature came from skeletons excavated from archaeological sites, or from unknown bodies called John or Jane Does at the morgue. In the early half of the 20th century, the most widely used means of determining stature was based on an early French study that consisted of a few dozen patients from an insane asylum. For scientific studies to be considered valid, they need to be based on large numbers of individuals. And for accurate results, a study should include bodies that are well documented with the known age at death, as well as the height and health of the person. The end of World War II offered the first major opportunity to study large numbers of well-documented bodies because every soldier had a complete and accurate health record. Sadly, one hour of battle during World War II supplied more than enough bodies for years of research.

Since the 1840s, the U.S. government has made it a priority to recover its soldiers killed in battle. For the first time, during the Spanish-American War, the government had to *repatriate* its servicemen, which meant bringing them home from foreign lands. During World War I, the Graves Registration Service was created to recover and identify the remains of dead American soldiers, but it was not until World War II that the army was put in charge, and physical anthropologists were employed to conduct the bulk of the work. The savage battle in the Pacific meant that many bodies were left behind in the field. Often the remains of Japanese and Koreans were jumbled in with American dead, and they needed to be separated and returned to their homelands. Temporary identification labs were set up as needed in Japan, South Vietnam, and Thailand.

The first woman to head the repatriation effort was Mildred Trotter, physical anthropologist and professor of gross anatomy at Washington University, St. Louis. In 1948, she was asked to organize and manage the lab in Hawaii where she was in charge of identifying the dead from some of the worst battles in the Pacific, including those that took place on Iwo Jima, on Guadalcanal, and in the Philippines. Many of the bodies brought into the lab had no identifying characteristics, and it was her job to examine the bones and come up with an identification based on X rays, dental charts, and health records supplied by the army and relatives of the deceased.

While working on the identification of the war dead, Trottter saw an opportunity of a lifetime. She knew that the charts and mathematical tables used to estimate the stature were old and based only on European men. They were not very reliable for estimating the height of an

American soldier. She had to convince her military superiors that it was important to the science and to the repatriation effort to amass large amounts of data that would be used to configure new stature charts and tables that would be more accurate than using 50-year-old data based on French men. She and her staff measured 790 male skeletons, most of whom were white. Only 80 were of African-American descent. Her work became the basis for the regression tables that American forensic anthropologists use today to estimate height from bones. She updated them with data collected in the 1950s from American soldiers in the Korean War, which included a greater mix of ethnic backgrounds, making the tables more comprehensive.

On assignment for the U.S. Army, anthropologist Dale Stewart and his men worked for four months in a smelly warehouse on the Japanese island of Kyushu surrounded by stacked boxes full of the bones of American soldiers. Stewart's research of 450 remains resulted in the method used today to estimate a skeleton's age at death based on the amount of bone growth between the knobby ends of the long bones and the shaft of the long bones.

The repatriation efforts continue at the Central Identification Laboratory in Hawaii, as does the research on which the field of forensic anthropology is based. For the past 50 years, the painstaking work of identifying military personnel from their bones is responsible for training most of the prominent forensic anthropologists working with law enforcement today.

THE FORENSIC TEAM

Forensic science is the link between the criminal and the crime.

—K. W. Goddard, *Crime Scene Investigations,* 1977

In the United States, the law protects all known or suspected human remains, and there are legal procedures for handling them. For example, if the manner of death is unknown or suspect, the coroner or medical examiner (ME) must be called in to investigate or perform an autopsy, which is a medico legal exam of the body to determine the cause of death. But this was not always the case.

The office of coroner was a holdover from an antiquated system that began in England in 1194 when the king decreed that every English county should elect three knights and a clerk to perform the duties of the office of coroner. Their main purpose was to collect taxes. If a murder victim was not an Englishman, a "murdrum" fine was collected. Even after the death tax was abolished, the coroner still showed up when a person died to help solve any disputes as to the cause of death. A coroner acted more as a judge with the authority to inquire into the cause of death of a person whose death was unexplained or suspicious. These coroners had no medical training, and the United States adopted this system, which lasted for centuries.

During the colonial period, coroners held inquests to judge the cause of death. In 1637, the coroner Thomas Baldridge impaneled a

The Medical Forensic Team

Coroner an elected or appointed official with no prerequisite training. He or she has the legal authority to investigate deaths.

Medical Examiner an appointed or hired position with investigative powers. The ME is required to have medical training and, in some areas, a pathology degree.

Forensic Pathologist sometimes holds the office of medical examiner and has a medical degree. A forensic pathologist's education includes graduate work in pathology, study of the diseases of the flesh, and at least one year of approved forensic training or two years of forensic experience.

Forensic Anthropologist requires a Ph.D. in physical anthropology (the study of the human body) with a solid background in biology, anatomy, physiology, osteology, chemistry, and archaeology. To be eligible to take the board certification exam requires a minimum of three years of experience in forensic work.

jury, which resulted in this verdict: "John Bryant by the fall of a tree had his bloud bulke broken; and hath two scratches under his chinne of the left side, and so that by means of the fall of the said tree upon him the said John Bryant came to his death." The first autopsies were being performed in Massachusetts by 1647, when the courts decreed that for teaching purposes "an autopsy should be made on the body of a criminal once in four years."

In the early 1900s, New York State had a wide assortment of unqualified men who held the job of coroner, including eight undertakers, seven politicians, six real estate agents, two bar owners, two barbers, one butcher, and one milkman. Perhaps the most qualified were the undertakers and maybe the butcher.

Today, there is no one system used by all states, counties, and municipalities. Some states still elect or appoint coroners, but most have retired the coroner system and have replaced it with a trained medical examiner. Like the coroner, the medical examiner has the power to investigate a death, but he or she is required to be a physician, a pathologist, or, in some areas, a forensic pathologist. The ME is required to appear at a scene of an unexplained death or is called in by the police when foul play is suspected. Medical examiners observe the area, judge the time since death, and take charge of the body, which is taken back to the morgue for an autopsy.

Working within the System

Ideally, there should be much communication between the police, medical examiner's office, and forensic anthropologist. Some law enforcement agencies, such as the FBI, have working relationships with academic institutions or museums, while smaller agencies like the Erie County Sheriff's Department in New York State have a forensic anthropologist on call as a scientific consultant. But in many areas of the country this is not the case. Many states could use a full-time forensic anthropologist, especially those in the south where decomposition is swift and skeletons accumulate. According to William Maples, former director of the C. A. Pound Human Identification Laboratory in Gainesville, Florida, the murder rate in Florida is high enough to keep six forensic anthropologists busy year-round.

The medical examiner and forensic anthropologist essentially perform the same duties—to examine the body and render a report on determination of identity and cause of death. Forensic pathologists, however, are trained in diseases and injuries of the flesh, while a forensic anthropologist specializes in the diseases, injuries, and variations of the human skeleton. So when a body's organs are badly decomposed, burned, or dismembered, and the skin is sloughing off and no longer useful for fingerprinting, a forensic anthropologist must be called in order to glean the most information from the remains. Most forensic anthropologists consider themselves on call 24 hours a day, but a body that needs the expertise of a forensic anthropologist is not usually one that is considered an emergency.

In 1996, a total of 1,439 forensic exams were reported on by certified forensic anthropologists. Eighty-one percent of those cases were examined at the request of a legal agency (local, state, federal law enforcement agencies, military, coroner, or medical examiner). Nineteen percent involved a civil dispute. Of those cases that came from law enforcement, 73 percent were examined at the request of a medical examiner or a coroner. Thirteen percent came from the military.

The study further explained that 23 percent of those cases were "fresh" or "fully fleshed" and 24 percent were decomposed remains. The majority of the cases, 31 percent, were skeletal remains with which forensic pathologists lack sufficient familiarity to make a comprehensive and informative *postmortem* examination. Often times, the pathologist's autopsy procedures run contrary to the forensic anthropologist's methods and can even destroy valuable osteological evidence.

Autopsy

The primary evidence in most medico legal cases is the body itself, and the principal investigative tool is the autopsy, which literally means "self-examination." A better term is necropsy, which means an examination of death (from the Greek word *necros*).

In a well-run medical examiner's system, the body of a person whose death is suspect is examined at the scene by the medical examiner or forensic pathologist. The body is placed in a body bag, and the evidence is sealed and transported to the medical examiner's office where it is logged in to preserve the chain of custody for the evidence. Once on the lab table, the seal on the body bag is broken and the medical examiner begins to record his or her observations of the appearance of the body and clothing. The clothing is removed one article at a time as the condition and markings, such as rips, knife cuts, or bullet holes, are described in detail.

The appearance of the body is also recorded, noting wounds, surgical scars, blood smears, and identifying features. The pathologist looks for any external symptoms that might point to cause of death, such as

Anthropologist Kathleen Arries examines skeletal remains in an autopsy room. (Kathleen O. Arries)

color changes associated with carbon monoxide, needle marks, or blunt-force trauma injuries. Photographs and X rays are taken. Trace evidence, such as material under the fingernails and swabs from the body's orifices, are collected. Blood and urine samples that might indicate poisoning are collected. After all trace evidence is recorded, the body is washed, and a second visual inspection of the cadaver is made before the surgical aspect of the autopsy is performed.

The first cut is a Y-shaped incision that begins at the shoulders and runs diagonally and downward to the sternum, or breastbone, and straight down to the pelvis. The skin and muscle are pulled back. The sternum and a section of the ribs are removed. The pathologist looks internally for the possible cause of death. Each organ is removed, weighed, inspected, and a section is saved for later microscopic analysis. The lungs, for example, are inspected for fluid that might have entered during a drowning. An enlarged or swollen heart might indicate an electrical shock, or the liver might reveal how much poison was administered to the victim. Examining the stomach contents and judging the rate of digestion helps to determine the time of death. Abnormalities such as stomach ulcers, kidney stones, and signs of arthritis are compared to the victim's medical records.

The forensic pathologist makes an incision in the scalp and pulls the skin back to reveal the skull. Using an oscillating saw, the top of the skull is removed. The brain is taken out and weighed, sampled, and its condition recorded.

When the autopsy is over, the organs are placed back in the chest cavity, and the incisions are closed. From these procedures, it is possible for the forensic pathologist to determine cause and manner of death. Cause refers to the actual event that precipitated the death. It might be a gunshot wound to the chest resulting in bleeding to death or asphyxiation due to smoke inhalation from a fire. The manner of death involves how the injuries occurred and who was responsible. Who pulled the trigger? How did the fire start? Was it accidental, suicide, homicide, or a natural death?

Depending upon the circumstances, a whole team of special investigators can be called upon to give their expert analysis of the evidence. Toxicologists conduct chemical analysis for the presence of poisons or drugs. Forensic odontologists examine the dental remains to verify identity, and criminalists analyze everything from fingerprints to firearms and interpret bloodstain patterns. If the body is unidentified or in such a condition—decomposed, skeletonized, or fragmentary—that the normal procedures of an autopsy would not reveal much information, a forensic anthropologist is called in. After a pathologist has examined the remains and taken any tissue samples for testing, the forensic anthropologist is free to examine and clean the bones, which are soaked in a bath of chemicals and hot water, a process that may take as long as three days for the flesh to be free from an entire body. Whatever the forensic anthropologist learns from the examination is sent to the medical examiner, who is the only one authorized to pronounce the cause and manner of death and sign the death certificate.

IS IT HUMAN?

Context can often play an important role in confusing even the best of us.

—Douglas Ubelaker, Smithsonian Institution

What happens when all that remains of a person are small bits of bone sealed in a Ziploc bag? The first question that must be asked is "Is it human?" That is the kind of question that causes most medical examiners to pause and turn to their Rolodex to call a forensic anthropologist.

Human bones that are whole and *articulated* (still attached to one another) are easy to identify, especially if it's a skull, but when bones are broken or burned and the *epiphyses* (the bony caps of the *long bones*) have been chewed off by wild animals or cut off by a murderer the job of identifying them gets more difficult.

Delaying a call to an anthropologist has, occasionally, led to unnecessary media frenzy and panic. When a hiker reported seeing a skeleton on a mesa west of Albuquerque, New Mexico, a sheriff's deputy was sent to investigate. What he found was a pile of bones mostly held together by desiccated tendons. There was no skull, and the torso was separated from the extremities. A pathologist should have been called immediately, but the remains were taken instead to a local physician, who judged it to be the right size for a 12-year-old child. From that bit of information, the report grew to a story about a 12-year-old girl having been raped, murdered, and dismembered. It was the headline story in every newspaper and the lead report on television newscasts. After three days, the remains were taken to the forensic pathologist who counted the rib bones and discovered that there were more than the normal number for a human body. When the forensic anthropologist arrived, he examined the bones closely for the first time since their discovery and observed cut marks on the neck vertebrae, where someone had severed the head from the body, and markings at the ends of the *phalanges*, the finger bones, where someone had, in this case, removed the claws from the paws. These were the remains of a young bear.

According to forensic anthropologist Douglas Ubelaker, between 10 and 15 percent of the cases sent to the FBI that are presumed to be human skeletal remains turn out to be some other kind of animal. Weeding out that 10 to 15 percent saves taxpayers' money and the police hours of tedious investigation.

During his tenure at the Smithsonian, Larry Angel had an alarming way of testing whether the small fragments that agents brought him were bone or stone. He would lick them. Small bone fragments often get mixed up with bits of rock and can be difficult to differentiate. By touching the fragment to his tongue, Angel could tell which bits needed his attention and which could be tossed in the trash. Bone will stick to the tongue because it is porous, but rock will not.

"Is it human?" is a legal question. Every human bone that is found must be investigated as thoroughly as possible. A civil case of accidental or natural death affects insurance claims, wills, and the financial matters of the deceased and his or her family. A criminal case could result in the capture and conviction of a murderer or even a serial killer.

Kathleen O. Arries, a forensic anthropologist on the sheriff department's scientific staff in Erie County, New York, says that when a bone comes in from the police department she just has to "eyeball it," but eyeballing in forensics means she has to know her bones, both human and nonhuman. Expertise in both human and nonhuman anatomy is one of the important and unusual strengths of the forensic anthropologist.

At a glance, Arries may notice that the rib bone is too large or the skull fragment is too thick to be human. She then compares the unknown bones to her reference collection, which is a set of skeletons of animals common to the area. Arries's collection consists of roadkills, dead animals found in the woods, and donations from her local butcher. Each skeleton is cleaned and set out to bleach on her back porch. If the suspect bone is not matched to one in her collection, she consults other specialists, such as an ornithologist, who studies birds, or a mammologist, who studies mammals.

If Arries thinks a bone, such as a fragment from a skull, may be human, she may try to fit the bone to a human reference skull, trying to match the contours of the bone fragment with those on the complete skull. If there are many fragments, she first must piece them together like a three-dimensional jigsaw puzzle.

The epiphyses of the long bones are good indicators of humanness because of the angle of the joint. Our leg bones are attached to the pelvis at an angle to allow us to walk upright on two legs, unlike animals that walk on all fours. If the epiphyses have been broken off and only the shaft of the bone called the diaphysis is left, then a close look at the inside of the bone will give a clue as to what kind of animal it came from.

Bone is not solid, but has a dense and hard outer layer with a spongy interior. The thickness of the outer layer, called the *cortex*,

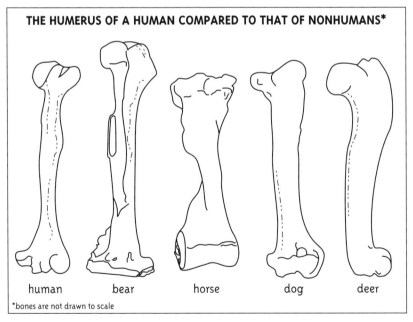

THE HUMERUS OF A HUMAN COMPARED TO THAT OF NONHUMANS*

human   bear   horse   dog   deer

*bones are not drawn to scale

This diagram shows the humerus of a human compared to those of a bear, horse, dog, and deer. Bones out of context are hard to identify. Comparing them to similar bones from other species shows how different the human anatomy is.

compared to the thickness of the total bone can indicate whether a bone is human or nonhuman. In an adult human, the cortex is roughly one-fourth the total thickness of bone. Large mammals, such as a dog or bear, have a thicker cortex, one-third the total diameter. Birds have thin bones. The cortex of a bird is only one-eighth the total diameter of the bone.

Inside living bone there is a spongy material called *cancellous tissue*. Within this tissue are *osteons* of the Haversian system. Osteons are round tunnels that hold blood vessels and nerve fibers and carry nourishment to the surrounding bone. In humans, osteons are scattered

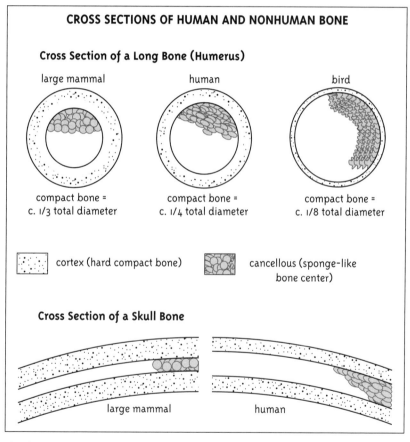

The thickness of the bone is one way to tell if it is human or nonhuman. In a large mammal the cortex is one-third the total diameter, and in birds the cortex is only one-eighth the total diameter of the bone.

randomly throughout the tissue. But in most animals the osteons are lined up in rows. Under the microscope, a wafer thin cross section of a nonhuman bone looks like a stack of bricks.

Sometimes it is this kind of microscopic evidence that reveals the distinction between a lying murderer and a messy hunter. A body of a woman was recovered from the bank of the Mississippi River. She was badly decomposed, but it was obvious that she had been shot in the chest. Police interviewed witnesses and tracked down a suspect who had been seen at a gas station washing out the front seat of his car. A forensic inspection of the suspect's car revealed blood on the floor mats and four small bone fragments, each less than an inch long. The suspect claimed he had been on a hunting trip and that the bones and blood were from a deer.

It was not possible to piece the tiny bone fragments to the victim's skeleton to prove that the bones were hers, but it was possible to look at the structure of the bones to see if they were human or that of a deer.

The state police located a recently killed deer for the experiment and took it to Douglas Owsley at the Smithsonian. Owsley carefully sliced a thin wafer of bone from the foreleg of the deer, as well as a cross section from the victim's humerus. Then, under a microscope, he compared the internal structures of the two bones to the internal structures of the bone fragments found in the car. The fragments did not resemble the osteon patterns of the deer bone, but they were similar to the bone structure of the murder victim. When the evidence was presented to the suspect prior to the trial, the man confessed that he had shot the woman as she sat in his car and rolled her body out of the passenger seat and into the river.

If there is any tissue left on a bone, a forensic anthropologist can use immunological tests to diagnose the species of a suspect bone. One case that was presented to the Smithsonian involved two partial skulls sent from the medical examiner in Oklahoma City. One skull had been brought up from the bottom of a freshwater lake, and the other had been found by an industrious dog in a town halfway across the state. They were calvarium skulls, or craniums that lacked facial bones.

The medical examiner had sent the bones out to several people resulting in several different tentative identifications, including that of an owl, a dolphin, and a deformed baby. The skulls were bulbous like a human's, but the occipital bone (the bone at the lower back of the skull) was not consistent with a human skull. Ubelaker consulted Hugh Berryman, a forensic anthropologist in Tennessee, who had seen a similar cranium. There were several features that suggested that they might be from a calf because one of the specimens had evidence of horn buds. But this was not a normal calf. Then Ubelaker remembered hearing from farmers that occasionally one of their cows would give birth to a calf with an enlarged and deformed cranium. Such a calf would not live more than a couple of days.

To test this theory that these were calf remains, Ubelaker removed a tiny piece of desiccated tissue and prepared it for an immunological test. Extracts from the tissue were tested with antibodies (proteins produced in the body that react with a foreign substance) of cattle, deer, horse, sheep, swine, and humans. It reacted positively with the cattle antibody. It was a calf.

Hands and Paws

In Colorado Springs, a dog happily gnawed on a bone, until the dog's owner, annoyed that his dog had gotten into someone's trash again, went to take the bone away. As the owner got closer, he saw that the dog was chewing on what looked like a human foot. The man called the police to investigate. It was indeed a foot, but there was no soft tissue left, and the last row of phalanges (finger and toe bones) were missing. It was hard to tell what kind of animal this foot had come from. The foot made the rounds at the local hospital, but no doctor was certain enough to say whether it was human or not. That evening the police launched a full-scale search throughout the neighborhood for the rest of the body.

Forensic anthropologist Michael Hoffman arrived the next morning to examine the bones. He saw that the foot was short, with no arch, and was missing not just one row of phalanges but two. He concluded that the foot was from a black bear, and the search for a murder victim was ended.

When a bear is skinned, the claws are removed by cutting off the first and sometimes the second row of phalanges, which shortens the feet, making them look remarkably like human hands and feet. But bears do not have opposable thumbs that can move and grasp. In anatomical position, which for humans is lying on the back with arms down at the sides, the hands are palms up. The anatomical position of a bear is standing up; paws are palms down. When positioned this way, the smallest digit of a bear paw is on the inside of the paw where our thumb is. This makes the bear paw a mirror image of human hands and feet. The right paw of a bear looks like the left hand and foot of a human.

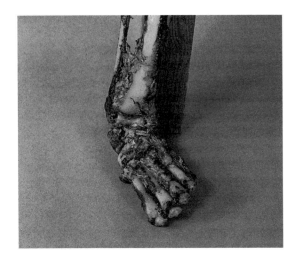

The skeletal foot of a bear that has had its claws stripped away looks remarkably like the foot of a human. (Kathleen O. Arries)

The case of the mistaken bear paw has been repeated more than once around the country. One case in Hamburg, New York, involved more than one foot. Two women out for a morning walk through a cemetery noticed a severed foot lying in the road. A search of the surrounding woods turned up eight more severed feet. The cemetery was cordoned off and the badly decomposed feet were sent to the medical examiner who, without the skull or long bones, could not tell right away whether they were human or nonhuman.

Kathleen Arries arrived on the scene and produced skeletal models of a human male foot and a human female foot from the trunk of her car. By comparing the severed feet to her reference skeletons she could tell they were not human, and later in the lab she determined they were from four different black bears, three immature and one adult. A local taxidermist was called in for questioning about the illegal shooting of a mother bear and her cubs.

Another case involving mystery bones dug from someone's backyard baffled two orthopedic surgeons, but the forensic anthropologist who examined them knew immediately that the charred bones along with a number of ribs and sacrum (lower vertebrae) were part of an animal's tail. There was no murder victim, just the leftovers of a pig roast.

Medical doctors and medical examiners are trained to deal with the human body fully fleshed, and they rarely see random loose bones of other animals. Forensic anthropologists see all kinds of animal bones frequently, even so, under some circumstances professional anthropologists can be fooled too.

Horse Tails and Dog Bones

Dale Stewart was working at the Smithsonian when he received a small package of bones from the FBI. They were labeled finger bones, and Stewart, without questioning the label, agreed. As he was examining them he was puzzled about something. What animal did they come from? He sent them to a mammologist who determined that the bones came from a horse. They were not finger bones at all but the tailbones of a horse.

The last vertebrae in a horse's tail is similar in size and shape to human phalanges, with one subtle difference. The ends of the vertebrae are flat and sharp-edged, whereas human finger bones are rounded at the top and bottom.

Knowing too much about a case can alter the way a specimen is examined, as Stewart found out by assuming the bones were finger bones instead of starting from scratch. Dr. Ubelaker makes a practice of protecting himself from any extraneous information or assumptions the police may have about a case. Sometimes he isn't always successful.

One day a package from an FBI agent arrived on Ubelaker's desk. It contained a bone that had been found at a campsite in Anchorage, Alaska. The bone itself had been badly broken and chewed on by several wild animals, and it would have been chewed to bits had it not been for the metal prosthesis embedded in it. The metal plate was the kind used to correct pseudoarthrosis, a condition in the elderly where a broken bone is too weak to mend itself. The metal plate is attached to the bone to give it support.

No orthopedic surgeon in Alaska could identify the workmanship, so it was sent to Ubelaker. Because of the metal plate, Ubelaker, like the FBI agents and the Alaskan doctors, assumed that the bone was human. It wasn't until he took a small sample of the bone and looked at it under the microscope that he saw the telltale animal pattern of osteons all stacked up like bricks. Although the prosthesis was the same make as those used in people, it had been implanted by a veterinarian in a large dog.

There are a number of animal bones that are routinely mistaken for human remains, such as the foot bones of a polydactylous pig (a pig with five toes) or the rib cage of a sheep. Many times the circumstances in which suspect bones are found are more important than the bones themselves. We are all used to seeing chicken bones on our dinner plate, but we would think twice if we saw them poking out from under our neighbor's new rosebush. In a forensic context, many animal bones are mistaken for human remains. In the right or perhaps wrong context, even the fin of a small whale can be mistaken as a human hand.

Once a case comes to the attention of the police, it has to be thoroughly checked out no matter how bizarre, and it is not enough to say that a bone is not human. The forensic anthropologist has to name the species. Eighty-five to 90 percent of the time the species turns out to be human, and then the real search begins. But without a forensic anthropologist's expertise in the bones of many different species, a potential investigation might get a false start. Being able to answer the question "Is it human?" allows a forensic anthropologist to point the police in the right direction—to either call off a search or go back to the site where the remains were discovered and examine the crime scene.

CRIME SCENE

The best case is not the one that brings reporters to the door . . . It is the case that sends the forensic anthropologist knocking at the door of the unknown.

—Stanley Rhine, University of New Mexico

Anthropology is an odd conglomerate of four basic fields: ethnology, the study of the behavior of living people; linguistics, the study of language, its variation, and origin; physical or biological anthropology, the study of the variation and evolution of human anatomy; and archaeology, the study of past peoples.

Physical anthropologists branch off into equally various fields, which include the study of how diseases have affected cultures past and present, primate studies, and the origin and evolution of man. The forensic branch deals with skeletons of recent origin.

It is this interesting mix that makes anthropologists so uniquely qualified to participate in forensic work. Their training in archaeological survey techniques, in particular, gives them a good eye for locating areas of human activity, habitation, and burials. And their excavation skills assure comprehensive recovery of human remains as well as other pertinent evidence in and around the crime scene. Even the most skilled police investigators often miss important evidence simply because they are not as familiar with human anatomy or lack the ability to recognize significant changes in the landscape that might indicate foul play. They may, for example, miss the clues of altered vegetation and stunted tree growth, which might indicate that a burial was present, or not look for important identifiers like dental fillings that might have been lost when a tooth exploded in a murderer's attempt to destroy a body in a fire.

Most forensic anthropologists have experienced the frustration of having to examine human remains that arrive in a box at their office and remind police officers that they can only report on what is available to them. They can't be sure whether missing bones were removed by a murderer, dragged away by a scavenging animal, or were overlooked by a sloppy recovery team. Forensic anthropologist Dennis Dirkmaat of Mercyhurst College, who encourages his fellow scientists to go to the crime scene, acknowledges the fact that a forensic anthropologist can wait for the bones to arrive in the office and adequately determine age, sex, and stature, but if the forensic anthropologist is at the scene, context can say a lot more. In addition to a basic anthropological profile, the forensic anthropologist can determine cause and manner of death and piece together what happened to the body after death.

There are many different types of crime scenes, but most of the bodies that are examined by forensic anthropologists are found in rural settings by hikers, hunters, or dogs intent on dragging home something good to chew. A body in an urban area is usually found much faster because of the odor of decomposition, so many of the cases forensic anthropologists work on begin when someone makes a shocking discovery.

Search and Recovery

The bones were loosely scattered in a thick stand of oak, maple, and beech trees, and three children, who had been out playing near their Pennsylvania home on that September afternoon in 1989, did not know what they were looking at until they saw the chalky white globe of a human skull. Without touching a thing, they ran home to get help. Their parents did not believe that the children had found a body, but the next morning they went to see for themselves, then quickly called the police.

Before the police arrived, they had a suspicion of who the person might turn out to be. Back at the station there was a report of a missing woman from New York State, but before they could confirm it they had to collect the remains. The skeleton was incomplete. Most of it was lying in a creek bed, but flowing water, soil erosion, and rodents had spread the bones over a wide area. As many of the bones as possible had to be found in order to make a positive identification. The police also needed other evidence that might have belonged to the victim or the murderer in order to piece together what happened.

The skull the children found was taken back to the medical examiner's office, where a forensic odontologist compared the dentition (arrangement of teeth) with the dental records of the missing woman from New York. They matched. The woman in the woods was from western New York. She had disappeared 16 months earlier while on a lunch break from the printing company where she worked.

Kathleen Arries was called in to assist in the recovery of all the bones and evidence. Her skills at archaeological excavation were designed to get the most information from the ground with as little disturbance of the site as possible. A forensic site is more or less treated like an ancient archaeological site. It is methodically mapped, photographed, and every artifact is cataloged so that police officers can reconstruct the events that led to the death.

When Arries arrived at the edge of the woods, she stooped under the plastic yellow ribbon that warned POLICE LINE—STAY OUT. The yellow marker ran from the road into the woods, all the way to the ravine and up the opposite slope, marking the boundary of the search area.

The way a search is conducted is usually dependent on the land and weather conditions. In the dry scrub plains of the Southwest, a body may be sighted easily by a low-flying airplane, but in thick vegetation searchers usually form an evenly spaced line within voice and visual contact. Moving slowly, the line advances forward to the opposite side of the search area where they shift over, like a typewriter being kicked back, to walk slowly in the direction from where they started. This continues until something is spotted. All evidence is flagged and mapped. An anthropologist's map of the recovery scene begins with a datum point, the one spot from which all else is measured. This could be the edge of the road, a landmark such as a large tree, or the corner of a building. Once the body or parts of the body are located, the recovery phase can begin.

The area to be excavated in the Pennsylvania woods was marked off in 20-foot sections by string and wooden markers. Makeshift tables of plywood on wooden sawhorses were set up next to sifting screens, which are large square frames with window screening on the bottom to filter soil through. Workers from the local police agencies took turns searching through the underbrush for artifacts, anything human-made, such as a weapon, clothing, cigarette butts, or a footprint. Each item had to be marked with a wooden stake, photographed, and its position recorded on the map. Other workers emptied shovels full of earth onto the sifters, looking for smaller fragments of bone, teeth, or buttons that otherwise would have been overlooked. Sifting through dirt and debris might seem overly cautious, but it could reveal the one clue that points to a specific suspect or confirms a victim's identity.

One case in Florida hinged on locating a gold filling of a suspect in a fiery murder-suicide. More than 10,000 burned bone fragments were pieced together, but the tooth was not found. Archaeological experts were called in to sieve the entire site of the burned-out cabin with a $\frac{1}{8}$th-inch mesh screening. When nothing new was recovered, they sifted the material again using a finer screen of $\frac{1}{16}$th-inch mesh. As the ash was pushed through a second time, the gold filling was finally exposed, and the identity of the suspect was confirmed.

Even the smallest bone could be a clue to a murder. The small bones of the hands can reveal defense wounds, tiny cuts the victim received trying to ward off the slashes of a killer's knife by holding up the palms of his or her hands. The tiny wing-shaped bone deep in the throat, called the hyoid, is the only skeletal evidence of a strangulation. It is crushed when a person is strangled.

For eight days, Arries and the recovery crew worked at the wooded site invisible from the main road and only accessible by two dirt roads leading to a narrow grassy lane. The remains were scattered over an area measuring 200 feet by 300 feet of woods and creek bed.

After every piece of bone was recovered, the police started their reconstruction of the crime. It began on the path near the road where a cigarette butt was found. The killer had probably been smoking and dropped it when he got out of his vehicle. At the edge of the grassy lane, they found a .22 caliber shell casing, suggesting that the killer shot the victim then carried her or forced her to walk into the woods. Deeper into the stand of trees, an earring was recovered. Maybe the victim had struggled to get free. Down the sloping ridge were the remnants of her panty hose and the other earring, and closer to the creek was her jacket.

In the creek bed, where her body had been dumped, were the bones and the rest of her clothing. After her body had decomposed, the bones were spread by the running water more than 200 feet downstream. The small lighter-weight bones had traveled the farthest from the original site. The femur, fibula, and tibia, and the tiny foot bones were found on the opposite side of the path, carried there by rodents and other animals.

With the police detective's reconstructed crime scene, and with help from an informant, a suspect was arrested. The story the informant told the police about the events of that day matched the story told by the trail of artifacts. But all the evidence collected in the woods was still not enough for the case to go to trial. The suspected murderer was released, let go on a legal technicality.

Taphonomy

Occasionally when a neophyte police officer or someone out for a walk discovers a body that has decomposed and the bones have become separated, they suspect that a killer had dismembered the body and spread the remains to hide the crime. But it is more likely that a body found on the surface was affected by much more than just the killer's weapon. The study of what happens to remains after death, or what causes the remains to be found in a certain condition, is called *taphonomy*. Anthropologists are keen observers of changes that might occur due to the environment, scattering of bones by scavenging animals or the flow of water. Much of this postmortem alteration to the body can easily be mistaken as, or associated with, the cause of death.

Peter Andrews, the curator of paleoanthropology at the Natural History Museum in London, England, lives in a rural area of Wales where he conducts his research on scavenging patterns of animals. He leaves animal carcasses on the hillside near his home and observes what happens to them. Mice, fox, dogs, and even deer will pick up old bones and carry them off, scattering a skeleton over a great distance. Andrews records which animals are most likely to take various bones and how their chew marks vary.

Rodents, such as mice and rats, have a pair of front teeth shaped like little chisels, which leave parallel gouges on the long bones. They prefer to gnaw on the long bones in the same way most people eat corn on the cob, nibbling along sideways. If you were to bite into a thick bar of chocolate, the tooth marks left in the chocolate would be similar to the ones rodents leave on bone.

Foxes leave very different-shaped marks on bone. They prefer to chew on the knobby ends of the long bones the way dogs eat a soup

Rodent chew markings on bone [Kathleen O. Arries]

bone, propping the bone up between their paws, chewing off the ends, and boring small cone-shaped holes into the edges of the bone with their tiny, sharp canine teeth. Even deer and sheep will disturb a cache of bones. They break the bones open by stepping on them in order to get to the nutritious marrow in the center. In a forensic situation, an anthropologist would be able to determine whether an animal gnawed on the bones after death occurred or if a killer mutilated the body at the time of death, which is an important distinction to make.

One recent study conducted by Travis Pickering of Tulane University, New Orleans, reported the taphonomic process of carnivore voiding. Pickering's study, which used baboon rather than human cadavers, tried to answer the question of what happens to remains after they have been eaten by a carnivore—a common enough occurrence in Africa to warrant such a study. He fed baboon carcasses to leopards and spotted hyenas and recorded the identifiable remains in the subsequent scat and regurgitated material. He found that significant identifiable remains such as whole phalanges, intact skin, toes, and fingernails can be recovered. Fingers, in particular, with their fingerprints and rings can be useful in identifying human remains.

Buried Bodies

Not all bodies are found on the surface. Industrious killers intent on hiding their crime bury their victims. Sometimes the burial is accidentally uncovered by road construction, housing developments, or flooding water that erodes the soil away, revealing the secret underneath. But most buried bodies would never be detected without the help of an informant to lead the police to the site. Unfortunately, the informant's directions might be sketchy, misleading, or just wrong. It is hard for a person in a state of panic to remember precisely where a body may be in the middle of the night in a remote and unfamiliar area. Even with an informant's help, the police may not know what to look for when trying to find a burial site.

The Washington, D.C., police department received a phone call about the body of a woman who had been missing for eight months. The informant said the body could be found buried in a stand of overgrown bushes behind a high-rise apartment complex. The police, sure of the tip, called Douglas Owsley at the Smithsonian. When Owsley surveyed the area with the police, he could tell immediately that the body was not there because the soil in the area had not been disturbed.

The earth is made up of layers, or strata, of soil of different composition, color, and texture. The study of this layering is called stratigraphy, and geologists and archaeologists use it to age recovered fossils and artifacts. When the layers are dug into, the stratas are jumbled, mixing the darker soils from the bottom with the lighter-colored topsoil. The once compact earth is loosened and will not be as compact as the area around it. The change in soil color is one indication a burial is present, and another is a depression.

A murderer, in a hurry to cover up his or her crime, usually digs the smallest hole possible, just deep enough to hide the body, then makes it level with the ground so the dirty deed does not attract immediate attention. But over time the earth settles. The body underneath decomposes and becomes smaller. The burial site sinks, forming a noticeable depression. Frequently, a second smaller depression forms in the middle of the larger one when the body cavity, which was once bloated with gases, deflates and sinks.

The surface of the soil cracks and separates at a burial site as the moist earth from beneath the ground dries out by the exposure to the air. The plants that once grew in that spot are disturbed and die, or their growth is stunted. Weeds take their place. After many years, someone with an experienced eye can spot a burial because of the differences in the earth and foliage, which is why Owsley knew the thicket was untouched. The foliage and earth were consistent throughout the entire area.

More information from the informant led the police to the furnace room of the apartment building. There was a long retaining wall with sand behind it. Owsley crawled behind the wall and found the body. "I noticed a depression and a subtle mound in the sand. That's where she was." Had it not been for Owsley's experience in recognizing the subtle clues that indicate the presence of a burial, the police would have wasted valuable time digging in the thicket behind the building.

The techniques used to recover a buried body are different from those used to recover one on the surface. A team will dig down slowly with small tools, such as a mason's trowel, digging four inches (10 centimeters) at a time to take the whole area down in levels. This is done to preserve the integrity of the site and to be able to accurately record the location of any small items that might be buried with the body. All the soil at the burial site is sieved in order to recover small bones and other pertinent evidence. A forensic anthropologist will also collect soil samples near the body for later chemical analysis. Soil samples that include pollen and insect remains may aid in determining time since death by pinpointing the season or month the burial occurred. With careful excavation techniques, investigators can even determine what kind of tool was used to dig the grave. Shovel impressions are often preserved in the soft soil of the walls of the site, and footprints can sometimes be recovered from the floor of the grave.

When all the soil is removed, the surrounding area is lower than the body, which now appears to lie on a platform of earth. This gives the scientists easy access to the body, enabling them to kneel or walk around it while inside the grave. As the body is revealed, its position and condition are documented with photographs and notes and diagrams. If possible, the body is lifted out as a whole and placed on a gurney for transport back to the morgue. If the skeleton is very old, the bones are taken out one by one and packed in boxes, with special care taken to preserve fingernails, rings, skin, hair, and fibers. Packing of the bones is of special concern to the anthropologists because damage to the remains destroys potential evidence. Each bone is carefully wrapped in newspaper and properly labeled. A full inventory should arrive with the remains at the lab for the forensic exam.

The Forensic Response Team

Most anthropologists who are called to assist at a forensic site drop their academic work and look around their department for any available graduate students for assistance. In many forensic programs there is always at least one eager student on hand. But when William M. Bass III was head of the Tennessee Anthropological Research Facility, he created a more official arrangement with the formation of the first forensic anthropology response team in the country. The response team is made up of graduate students attending the forensic program at the University of Tennessee, and at any time there are four team members, two to put on gloves and handle the remains, one to take photographs, and one to record the procedures. They are on call 24 hours a day, seven days a week. They meet police at any site where an unidentified body has been or might be found, arriving in a truck fully equipped with a police radio, shovels, rakes, surgical tools, boots, gloves, and body bags.

Most of the cases that they respond to involve decomposed, unidentifiable bodies discovered along the highway by road crews or in the woods by hunters. The key word is unidentifiable. If the body still has fingerprints or can be visually identified by relatives, then the medical examiner is called. If a body's organs are decomposed and the skin is sloughing off, the forensic response team is called. Each year the response team exhumes buried remains, searches for and collects bod-

A police officer kneels at the edge of a shallow grave where the soil has been removed to reveal the remains of a woman. The polyester clothes are still intact after nine years in the ground.
(Kathleen O. Arries)

ies found on the surface, and participates in the identification efforts that follow a mass disaster.

In 1983, an explosion that rocked an illegal fireworks warehouse in rural Tennessee was so forceful that the tremors could be felt 15 miles away. The top priority for the response team was to collect and piece together the scattered human remains. For two grueling days they gathered body parts from the surrounding fields, loading them into two refrigerator trucks, one for bodies and one for parts. Dr. Bass, who worked the site, recalled that "we had a pile of shaved legs and a pile of unshaved legs." The team assumed that the shaved legs probably belonged to females and the hairy legs to males. When it came time to piece together the bodies, female legs were matched with female torsos, and male legs with male torsos. The team of graduate students learned that the limbs were very important because an identifying ring or bracelet would be recognized by a relative and clinch the identification.

Mass Disaster

A mass disaster is defined as a large number of dead at one time in a single location, but even unexpected situations arise that qualify for immediate help. For example, during the 1993 and 1994 floods in the Midwest, forensic anthropologists were asked to help identify the bodies inside caskets that floated up to the surface and were carried miles away by floodwaters. Nearly 800 caskets were disrupted, some of which were corralled and tied to boats that towed them to dry land. In a cemetery, the only means of identification is the headstone that stands firmly in the ground. The coffins and the bodies inside them are not marked with a name or even a plot number, so when they float to the surface they are indistinguishable. Many of them were dated by the type of coffin and the artifacts found with them. Within two weeks, the seven-person response team examined more than 400 individuals.

Many forensic anthropologists are familiar with working mass disaster situations, because they may be volunteers of the Disaster Mortuary Operation Response Team, also known as DMORT, which was formed in 1992 as part of the United States Public Health Service Office of Emergency Preparedness. DMORT was originally a mortuary service but grew to include scientific specialists who could aid in identification. The diverse group includes forensic pathologists, medical examiners, forensic odontologists, funeral directors, medical technicians, radiologists, mental health practitioners, and computer specialists who, when activated, all become temporary employees of the federal government.

There are 10 regional DMORT divisions located around the country. Forensic anthropologist Frank Saul is regional commander of DMORT V, which covers several states, including Ohio, Michigan, Wisconsin, Indiana, and Missouri. The 200 members of DMORT V are specialists in their field and have trained at least once a year in various emergency situations. In 2000, DMORT V participated in a mock terrorist bombing staged at the General Motors (GM) headquarters in Detroit, Michigan. The team members also cross-train in order to assist other specialists in their job; so that a mortician, for example, would feel comfortable recording the observations of a forensic anthropologist.

DMORTs are activated after natural disasters and major calamities, such as the bombing of the Alfred Murrah Building in Oklahoma City. But most often they are called upon to help recover and identify the passengers and crew members who die in aviation accidents, such as the crash of TWA Flight 800 in 1996, Con Air crash in 1997, and United Airlines Flight 93, which went down in a Pennsylvania coalfield on September 11, 2001.

Crash Site

The procedures for responding to and working an aviation crash site have been honed over the years, so when the response crews descended on the crash site outside the little town of Shanksville, Pennsylvania, they knew what they needed to do. However, they were daunted by the extensive damage to the plane and passengers. According to investigators, the flight hijacked by terrorists was wrestled out of terrorist control by passengers on the plane—its hijacked destination unknown. The plane suddenly took a nosedive, accelerating to 200 mph. When the plane hit the ground, its impact carved out a V-shaped gash and a giant crater 20 feet deep. According to one investigator, "The plane was pretty much disintegrated. There's nothing left but scorched trees."

Forensic anthropologist Dennis Dirkmaat, who works closely with the Pennsylvania coroner's office, responded to the crash site almost immediately, followed by other forensic investigators activated through DMORT. Dirkmaat had devised the protocol based on archaeological techniques to work a site such as this. The area was marked off in a grid of 20 square yards, and investigators examined each section by walking shoulder to shoulder across the site. They marked pieces of wreckage, personal effects, and human remains with a different colored flag. Each item was then photographed and recorded in a logbook before it was bagged and numbered.

All human remains were taken to a temporary morgue set up in a nearby armory. Each bit of tissue was accompanied by data collection forms that were filled out by the examining specialist at each successive station. Dirkmaat determined the anthropological description of the remains, while a pathologist wrote a pathological description. The remains were then photographed and x-rayed. "In a crash like this we saw extreme fragmentation," Dirkmaat said.

But the process of identifying the fragments would be made simpler by the fact that the airlines provided a complete manifest to work from. The forensic investigators in New York City did not have that luxury.

The Largest Crime Scene

The crime scene that used to be the World Trade Center was many times larger and more complicated than the Pennsylvania site, because no one knew how many victims there were or who they were. The New York City morgue was capable of handling up to 200 bodies, but the list of suspected victims was so large that a temporary morgue was set up in a hangar at La Guardia Airport. A convoy of 10 refrigerated tractor trailer trucks, draped with American flags, were parked outside of the medical examiner's office on First Avenue and Thirtieth Street. The city ordered 30,000 body bags, and a barge—carrying pallets of ice to keep remains from decomposing—to be unloaded at the nearest pier.

The magnitude of this disaster could not be compared with anything in the past. The Oklahoma City bombing killed 168 people, and the crash of American Airlines Flight 191 in Chicago—the most destructive aviation accident in the United States prior to September 11—killed 273. But in just 48 hours of the twin towers' collapse more than 4,000 people were reported missing and the numbers grew. The total count fluctuated as duplicate names were crossed out and new victims were reported. Six weeks later authorities reported 4,136 victims, including the 157 passengers and crew members aboard both airplanes, but the official figure after six months was fixed at 2,823 people lost on that day.

Early work at the site was organized as a rescue mission. Heavy construction equipment was not allowed to move the debris before it was first searched for survivors. Hundreds of rescue workers scooped up debris with their hands and filled bucket after bucket that were passed down a 200 feet bucket-brigade line to be emptied in front of FBI investigators who sifted through it for evidence. Workers on the site did not find as many intact bodies as they thought they would, instead, they found fragments—just an arm, a bit of flesh, or a tooth. Each bit was placed in a separate bag to avoid contamination with other remains and then taken to one of several staging areas near the site before being transported to the medical examiner's office.

As weeks wore on, debris was trucked to a remote area of the Fresh Kills Landfill on Staten Island, where FBI agents, police investigators, and firefighters wearing biohazard suits, respirators, and boots sorted through it with garden rakes. Ash was sifted through screening to find teeth and bits of bone. "It was an eerie, otherworldly place," said forensic anthropologist Julie Saul. She sorted bits of debris on the night shift under an old M.A.S.H. tent. The landfill was lit by floodlights. It was cold and rainy, and workers stood in puddles that were bubbling with methane gas.

The amount of debris precluded any attempt at a detailed scientific search, except for the fact that it was emptied and sorted by sectors. Huge cranes and excavating equipment the size of houses moved the piles, and any evidence that was found was taken to investigators inside one of several tents. Identification such as credit cards or ID tags were sent to the FBI tent. Pieces of fire-fighting equipment or uniforms were taken to the firefighter's tent. Anything that looked human was taken to where Saul worked her 7 P.M. to 7 A.M. shift. "A lot of it was food," she said. It came from dozens of restaurant freezers and refrigerators; racks of lamb, whole turkeys, stuff from garbage cans, the laundry, and everyone's bagged lunch confused the search.

"And the extreme heat did strange things to plastic, twisting it into weird shapes," said Saul. "It was up to us to separate out what was human." The flow of material was slow and sporadic. Some sectors did not have anything human, consisting primarily of building material, but occasionally the search crews would hit a pocket of human remains.

Forensic specialists worked around the clock tending to the hundreds of numbered body bags brought in daily to the medical examiner's office by ambulance and morgue wagons from the World Trade Center site and the landfill. The few intact bodies that were found in the first few weeks of the recovery effort were autopsied by forensic

Search-and-rescue dogs maneuver through the World Trade Center site trying to catch the scent of victims buried under the debris. Discovered remains are taken to one of several staging areas to be assessed before being sent to the morgue for identification. [FEMA]

pathologists. Radiologists took X rays of body parts, and forensic dentists looked at dental remains. Forensic anthropologists examined the severely burned remains and fragments to identify what parts of the body they may have come from and wrote a biological profile—sex, age, ancestry, stature, and body use—for each "remain unit." Other DMORT members collected antemortem information from family members, entered information into the computer systems, or took genetic samples from victim's relatives.

By late October, less than 200 intact bodies had been recovered, but more than 8,000 body parts and bits of tissue were brought back to the morgue. After six weeks, 425 people were identified using fingerprints and dental X rays, but the job of identification would take many months. It would also take expert knowledge about death, decomposition, and the human body.

6

THE BODY FARM

You decompose much more slowly in Minnesota than you do in Miami.

—William M. Bass III, University of Tennessee

Bodies lying out in the open, sunk into a murky pond, and buried in shallow graves in the woods behind a university hospital recall a scene right out of a fictional horror movie, but this scene is real. It is called ARF, the Anthropological Research Facility, or as some of the founder's colleagues call it, the Bass Anthropological Research Facility, BARF.

William M. Bass III first started working at the University of Tennessee in the anthropology department in 1971. He quickly gained a reputation as a bone expert, receiving calls from police departments all over the country, and whenever Bass arrived at a homicide scene, the first question the police would ask him was how long had the body been there.

In 1977, Bass was asked to examine a body that had been discovered lying in a disturbed grave at a historic cemetery just outside of Nashville, Tennessee.

Bass met the police at the cemetery, and with someone holding on to his ankles, he lowered himself headfirst into the grave. The remains he saw were clothed in pieces of tuxedo, and the right hand of the cadaver still wore a white glove. A pungent odor rose up from the body to greet Bass, and pink flesh and intestines were clearly identifiable. When Bass was hauled out of the grave, he pronounced judgment. The victim was a white male, 25 to 28 years at time of death, which occurred six to 12 months before.

More research on the case eventually yielded a positive identification. The man was Colonel William Mabry Shy, indeed a white male who died when he was 26 years old. But, he was shot in the head during the Civil War in the Battle of Nashville in 1864.

"I only missed it by 113 years," Bass joked. He had misjudged the time since death for several reasons. Shy's body was remarkably preserved because he was one of the first people ever to be embalmed in Nashville, and his coffin, which was made of cast iron, had been airtight until grave robbers broke into it. But Bass had also misjudged the time since death, or the *postmortem interval*, because so little hard data was known about the processes of death. What happened to a body when it decomposed? Was the process sequential? Were decay rates predictable? No one had ever conducted such studies because squeamishness and traditional religious beliefs had impeded any real hard scientific research. Without a sound basis for judging crucial information, such as how long a person had been dead, the effectiveness of law enforcement to solve murder cases was diminished. Estimating the postmortem interval is one of the most important pieces of information that police ask the scientific community to supply. It can crack an alibi, eliminate a suspect, or place a victim in a suspect's presence.

Open-Air Research

The case of Colonel Shy made Bass think about how one could collect the data that would answer those kinds of questions. Eventually, he approached the University of Tennessee and requested space to put bodies. The university officials gave Bass a former dump site and an office tucked within the walls of the football stadium. Within a few months, the first body arrived, and the facility, which cops nicknamed the body farm, was created. Bass started by placing bodies on the ground of the two-acre wooded area, which is surrounded by a chain-link fence, topped with barbed wire, and a wooden inner fence to keep out curious students. Some bodies lie out in the open air, in the shade, or in the sun. Some are fully clothed, others are nude. They are placed on platforms, wrapped in blankets, or tucked into the trunk of a car. As each body decomposes, the changes are carefully observed and recorded. "It may be weird, but how else do you get it done?" Bass explains. "You can't theorize about it."

The first studies were simple, based on visual and olfactory observations. One forensic case Bass was called to assist with involved a skeleton discovered when a bulldozer cleared a vacant lot between two houses. The remains belonged to an elderly white male who had died of natural causes and decomposed hidden in the tall grass. Everyone was shocked. How could a body decompose for so long, so close to two occupied homes without anyone smelling it? To answer that question, Bass offered 10 points of extra credit to any anthropology student who would come out to the facility the following weekend. A decomposing body had been placed on the ground, and Bass had marked off distances in 10-yard increments around the remains. As the students approached the corpse, the question was answered. Humans can't smell a decomposing body from more than 30 yards away.

Working with dead bodies never bothered Bass. "It's a puzzle to me," he said, "a challenge to tell who it was, how it got there, and tell what happened to them." According to Dr. Bass, "When a body comes in, it becomes a research tool." It is a 206-piece puzzle from the 206 bones in the human body. Although Bass is still actively working forensic cases, he has passed on the key to the body farm to his successor and former student, Dr. Murray Marks, who is now curator. What at first appeared to be a bizarre experiment has since turned into the world's only laboratory for human decomposition studies. Since it opened, more than 300 people have decayed there in the name of science. Today, bodies come from three sources. They still receive cadavers that are unclaimed from the morgue, but they also accept bodies that are donated by relatives, and those that are preplanned. Some people have requested that when they die they want their remains to go to the body farm.

According to Marks, the facility "processes" 40 to 50 bodies a year, plus a number of dogs donated by the local animal shelter. "Processing" means letting the decomposition process take its natural course and watching what happens. Although much of the research is designed to generate basic data about the rate of decomposition, some projects attempt to duplicate specific forensic situations. In this sense, the research is driven by criminals and the law enforcement agents who investigate their crimes. As closely as possible, Marks and colleagues have recreated many different types of occurrences that are common in forensic work, such as bodies wrapped in plastic, buried in shallow graves, lying uncovered on the ground, on concrete slabs, and in the

Dr. William Bass examines a skull at the Anthropological Research Facility at the University of Tennessee. (Photo provided by the University of Tennessee)

trunks and backseats of cars. Each experiment offers a glimpse of how a body decays in a specific situation. Each day, graduate students record the appearance of the body and its decomposition, as well as the change in plant growth, soil conditions, weather, temperature, and the number of insects and their activities. This continues until the body is fully skeletonized.

Some experiments are designed to answer specific questions for the court. One case that was scheduled in an appellate court had so many discrepancies that the prosecutor contacted Dr. Bass for some answers. The man on trial had been convicted of a double murder 10 years previously, but contradictory reports stated that he shot the victims in the back, and another said he shot them in the chest. Dr. Bass found both reports equally confusing and set out to answer a few questions, such as what the damage to the sternum (breastbone) looks like when shot from the front versus the back. After examining a human sternum that he had shot in the chest, Bass concluded that the wounds inflicted on the two murdered men were similar to those he observed on the experimental breastbone. Bass's research shed new light on the case and also added new information about a bullet's impact on the sternum.

But the most important piece of information that Bass and his students have extracted from all of their research is the pattern of decay.

By recording all the subtle changes that occurred on the many bodies processed at the farm, a clear pattern emerged.

Early Postmortem Changes

Death is gradual. When the heart stops beating, and respiration ceases, the cells of the body begin to die from lack of oxygen. When the oxygen in the brain is gone, brain activity ceases as do reflexes. This is referred to as somatic death. Then muscle, tissue, and organ cells break down and die in a process that takes from a few minutes to a few hours. Pathologists have long recognized three conditions that occur early in the decomposition process, which can be used to determine the postmortem interval.

At the moment of death, the body begins to lose heat. This is called *algor mortis* (Latin for cold death). Theoretically, the body's core temperature, which in life is 98.6 degrees F (37 degrees C), falls approximately 1 to 1.5 degrees F per hour, and will continue to fall until the body is at the temperature of the surrounding environment. Judging the postmortem interval using algor mortis requires taking the body's temperature and comparing it to the ambient temperature of the environment. A formula frequently used subtracts the victim's rectal temperature from 98.6, and divides that by 1.5 to equal the approximate number of hours since death occurred.

But there are several factors that affect how fast or how slowly the body temperature drops: the temperature of the environment, the temperature of the body at the time of death, the size of the body, and clothing. A large body will lose heat more slowly than a small one, and a fully clothed body will retain heat longer than a nude corpse. In a cold climate, a body will lose heat faster than in a warm climate.

When the blood ceases to circulate, it settles in the parts of the body closest to the ground. As it pools, the blood also clots and turns a dark bruiselike blue. If a person died while lying face up, the blood would pool on the back, buttocks, and back of arms and legs. Tight clothing may restrict the settling of the blood, and these areas will become blanched, as would the parts of the body in contact with the ground. The victim on his back, for example, would develop white patches where the skin was in contact with the ground. This pattern of color becomes fixed and is referred to as *livor mortis* (Latin for bluish death), postmortem lividity, or hypostasis. The blood begins to settle as soon as the heart ceases to pump it through the system. The discoloration sets in within 15 to 20 minutes after death and is evident within one to two hours. The color pattern becomes fixed in place after four to six hours.

The extent of livor mortis is an indicator of time since death, but the pattern of discoloration is also a clue as to whether the body was altered after death. If the pattern of livor mortis does not correspond with the position that the body was found in, investigators can assume that the body was moved.

Because the blood is not circulating, the muscles are denied oxygen and lactic acid builds up in the tissues. A chemical reaction involving the proteins actin and myosin causes stiffness in the body called *rigor mortis* (stiff death). This rigidity begins in the small muscles of the face, the eyelids, and the jaw, and works its way throughout the whole body. Rigor begins within two to four hours after death, and theoretically an average body will be in a state of complete rigor within 24 hours. The stiffness will last for 36 to 48 hours, after which the chemical process begins to break down and the body becomes flaccid again. The extent of rigor is also dependent on physical and environmental factors. Hot weather as well as a fever will accelerate the onset of rigor, and it will last for a shorter duration. Physical activity just prior to death will also result in a faster onset. Heavier and sedentary bodies will be slower to stiffen up and rigor will last for a longer period of time.

The sooner a pathologist can examine a body for these three characteristics, the more accurate the postmortem interval estimate would be. But pathologists only see a single body for a short period of time. They don't keep them for prolonged studies. One day they see a three-hour-old body of an elderly male, the next they see a day-old body of a child. In this manner, over a course of a career, a pathologist develops a cross-sectional collage of the changes that occur after death, which allows him or her to accurately estimate the postmortem interval. But this kind of knowledge is not easily transferable to pathology students. At the body farm, however, students see the time line in its entirety. They are able to exam the same body on day one as on day 100. It is this continuity that has made the research at the body farm so unique, and it has enabled Bass and Marks to map the processes of decomposition from the first fly to dry bone.

Decomposition

During life, the gastrointestinal tract continuously produces a mucus that protects the living tissue from destruction, but after death the

Stages of Decomposition

Early Postmortem Decay Characterized by internal microorganism activity, insect activity, production of internal gases, and normal appearance of body.

Putrefaction Characterized by increased microorganism and insect activity, bloating from gas buildup, strong odor, and purge fluid.

Black Putrefaction Characterized by blackened flesh, strong odor, and the collapse of the body.

Butyric Fermentation Characterized by the fermenting of exposed flesh and the drying of tissues.

Dry Decay Flesh is leathery and hard.

Skeletonization Most of the soft tissue is gone, bones are almost completely exposed, and ligaments and cartilage may still be intact.

digestive enzymes continue to work without the normal controls of the living body. This process is called *autolysis*, meaning automatic digestion—the body feeds on itself.

Putrefaction, the major component of decomposition, is a bacterial action. Bacteria that normally live in the human body are like prisoners in a jail. They are kept alive but under control. Once the body dies, the jail bars disappear and the bacteria are freed. They reproduce quickly and feed on the soft tissues of the body, reducing them to a fluid. The bacterial action causes the formation of gases and the rotten-egg smell of sulfur. As the gases accumulate, the body becomes bloated until the pressure eventually collapses the surrounding tissue and leaks out in what is called purge fluid. Insects attracted to the body, come to feed on the flesh and lay eggs, which produce a progression of larvae that also feed on the tissue.

The skin blackens and this is known as black putrefaction, which is followed by butyric fermentation, a stage where the exposed flesh ferments and slowly dries. Advanced stages of decomposition result in a dry decay where the remaining tissue becomes leathery and hardened. When most of the soft tissue is gone and the bones are clearly exposed, then the body is considered skeletonized, even though ligaments and cartilage may still keep the bones articulated. Knowing this pattern, scientists can estimate the length of time a person has been dead by the degree to which decomposition has occurred.

Rate of Decay

Just as algor, livor, and rigor mortis are affected by the environment, so are the advanced stages of decomposition. The major variable is climate. Heat and humidity speed up the process of decay, and cold slows it down. In the heat of a Tennessee August, a body can be completely skeletonized in as little as two weeks, but in winter that same process can take months. So the pattern that has been established at the body farm is not a timetable but a sequence of what happens first, second, third, and so on. Although the baseline developed in Tennessee can be used fairly accurately to estimate the postmortem interval of a body found in similar climates, it has to be modified for use in other areas of the country. Additional forensic studies conducted by William Haglund are more applicable to the northwest, and research by Alison Galloway recorded the rate of decay in the desert southwest. A long-term project that Dr. Marks has been spearheading is the creation of a color atlas on decomposition that would become the gold standard for law enforcement. It would include a page by page, moment by moment, insect by insect depiction of decomposition on a temperature and time line. Investigators would simply need to look at the corpse and look at the atlas to determine at what stage of decomposition the remains were in.

Extreme climates such as a desert environment inhibit decay. The dry heat of the desert causes the water in the body to evaporate so quickly that there is not enough time for microbes and insects to act on it. The skin dries out in the heat in the same way that leather is made by tanning. The same process also occurs in extremely cold and windy places where bodies are freeze-dried. The wind and below-zero temperatures of the Alps preserved the body of a 5,000-year-old man so well that even the delicate tissue of the eyeballs was still intact.

Besides climate there are other factors that affect the process, such as the type of soil the body is found in. Bodies on the surface tend to decay faster than buried bodies, because insects that feed on the body have easy access. However acidic soils will acceler-

Factors That Accelerate Decomposition

Small body size

Open wounds

Exposed flesh

Warm, humid climate

Moist or acidic soil

Scavenging animals

Insect activity

Factors That Decelerate Decomposition

Large body size

Uninjured body

Clothing or wrapping

Container

Burial

Cold climate

Alkaline soil

Submergence in water (unless in the presence of scavenging aquatic animals)

ate the process of decomposition of a buried body, because the acid in the soil draws out the calcium phosphate from the bones. Bodies buried one to two feet underground may become skeletonized in a few months to a year, but the same process may take years for bodies buried deeper (three to four feet).

In slow-moving or standing water or even in extremely moist soil, fat on a body becomes saturated with moisture and the tissue turns into *adipocere*, which is a white waxy substance created by a chemical reaction with water that converts body fat to fatty acids. Once adipocere forms, it is relatively permanent, preserving bones for years. For example, the body of a man who died in 1792 had been so completely preserved by adipocere that it was on display in the Hall of Physical Anthropology in the National Museum of Natural History in Washington, D.C., for many years.

But some bodies that are pulled out of their watery graves are almost completely skeletonized because of aquatic scavengers called sea lice. These small crustaceans are only a quarter of an inch long, but they congregate in a cloud of thousands that can clean a body of its flesh in a matter of hours. Divers who recover drowning victims often have to be careful not to let the sea lice get on their skin. Not much has been known about underwater decomposition until recently when Gail Anderson, head of the forensic entomology laboratory at Simon Fraser University in British Columbia, submerged six pig carcasses in Howe Sound. Her studies will be used to develop a baseline for how saltwater creatures, such as crabs and shrimp, interact with dead bodies.

Sight, Smell, Touch

Once the tissue has decayed and only the bones are left, a lot can still be learned about time since death by what the bones feel like, look like, and smell like. A bone that has a greasy feel to it is called green bone and indicates a fairly recent find. Bones stay green above ground for less than a year, but buried bones can retain that greasy feeling for much longer. Bones left lying out on the surface become bleached white and brittle in the sun, losing all their moisture. Bones that have been buried become stained and dark. The color of the bone can indicate whether it has been moved or not. When a bleached white skull is dug from a shallow grave or dark-stained long bones are found in a pile above the ground, it's clear that the bones have been moved, intentionally or unintentionally. Exposure to freezing temperatures creates lacy cracking on the surface, indicating that the bones have weathered at least one winter. Even after all the soft tissue is gone, the long bones will still have a slight odor from the residue of bone marrow inside the bone cavity. It smells like candle wax, and the odor can linger for up to 50 years.

The Biochemistry of Decomposition

Today, graduate students at the body farm are as likely to collect data with a biopsy needle as they are to record the loss of tissue with pencil and paper. Dr. Marks, director of the research facility, says, "Bass was a pioneer of decomposition on the gross level, recording the observable changes that occurred. Now we are studying the biochemistry of those changes. Decomposition is not just a breakdown of material, it is a creation of new substances. New compounds are produced when a body's chemicals, which normally don't associate with each other, mix together due to the breakdown of the body."

It is this creation of chemicals, some of which are aptly named cadaverine and putriscine, which are measured. With a biopsy needle samples are taken from various major organs, such as the brain, liver, heart, and kidneys. These samples are analyzed with gas chromatography and mass spectrometry. Gas chromatography can identify the various compounds in a sample by exposing them to a solvent that separates each component, which become visible when a reagent is applied. To substantiate the results, the samples are subjected to mass spectrometry, which bombards the sample with a beam of electrons to shatter the material into its original components. The charged particles are then separated and quantified according to their atomic masses. Each compound has its own identifiable mass spectrometry pattern.

Marks and his colleagues are looking for biomarkers, which are chemicals that can be linked to a specific time or sequence of decomposition. They want to be able to say that given a specific set of circumstances, certain chemicals will be in the body at these levels at a particular time. In the future, Marks will be able to take a biopsy sample from a murder victim and read the biomarkers to determine the exact time since death. Soil samples taken from beneath a corpse are also being analyzed to identify by-products of decomposition that seep into the ground. Long after a body has been removed, researchers can determine from the soil samples how long it was lying in a particular location.

Some forensic anthropologists joke that they can tell how long a person had been dead by the time it takes the university staff to complain about the smell. But actually they are collecting hard data that might link those odors to a specific decomposition time frame. By using a machine that is essentially an electronic nose with 32 sensors, researchers can record the changes in odors. That information is then fed through a gas chromatograph to identify and quantify the distinct parts of the mixture. This information may someday help to train cadaver dogs to more effectively seek out buried murder victims or people who are trapped under debris after an avalanche, earthquake, or other mass disaster.

All of this may seem rather unpleasant, but the research at the body farm is conducted in the most serious manner, and the findings have important implications for future forensic work. Of the more than 60 forensic anthropologists currently working for law enforcement agencies, about one-third were trained at the research facility, as were many FBI agents and police cadets. The difficult task of determining how long a person has been dead has become more precise, and the more precise the forensic scientists are, the more successful the police are in catching killers.

7

THE BUG DETECTIVES

Insects are major players in nature's recycling effort, and in nature a corpse is simply organic matter to be recycled.

—M. Lee Goff, Chaminade University of Honolulu

Graduate students and police cadets are not the only visitors to the restful residents at the body farm. The first to arrive are insects. Within minutes after death and being exposed to the elements, the first flies arrive. From a mile away, gravid females, looking for a warm, moist place to lay their eggs, can sense the subtle chemical changes that occur at the moment of death. Within days, the body is swarming with maggots.

The connection between death and insects was recognized as far back as 1235. In the book *Washing Away of Wrongs*, the 13th-century Chinese investigator Sung Ts'u recounted how a magistrate used insect evidence to solve the murder of a man. The victim's wounds appeared to have been made by a rice sickle, so the magistrate ordered all the men to bring their tools and gather in the village. As they lined up, he watched the flies land on one particular blade, attracted by the almost invisible traces of the victim's blood and tissue. When the magistrate confronted the owner of the sickle, the man confessed to the crime.

Six hundred years later, in 1855, insects were key witnesses in another classic *forensic entomology* case. This time the victim was an infant who was discovered during the remodeling of a house outside of Paris. The small body had been sealed up behind a fireplace. The couple who had recently moved to the house were immediately under suspicion, but when Dr. Bergeret d'Arbois of Switzerland performed an autopsy on the tiny body, he discovered several generations of insect remains, which indicated that the body had been hidden for much longer than a year. He concluded that the child had been dead since 1848, long before the current owners took up residence. The former homeowners were eventually arrested and convicted of the murder.

Using insect evidence to solve a crime is called forensic entomology, and it has been practiced in one form or another in Europe for more than 100 years, but in the United States, insects are relatively new members of the forensic team. Their specialty is providing data to determine the postmortem interval.

Pig Research

Insects are predictable. A species tends to stick with one type of food or stay in one particular environment. Some lay eggs only at high noon or only in the shade. It is this predictability that makes them prime candidates for use in postmortem interval assessments. Research on human cadavers at the Anthropological Research Facility in Tennessee has proven that insects arrive at a corpse in a predictable sequence and are responsible for the majority of the tissue loss on a body.

Not all research, however, is conducted on human cadavers. Most insect research is done with dead pigs. M. Lee Goff at the Chaminade University of Honolulu and one of the founding diplomates of the American Board of Forensic Entomology uses 150-pound (70-kilogram) pigs because they are most like humans. A pig is not very hairy, has a similar intestinal tract, a similar diet, and it closely approximates the decomposition patterns of an adult human.

Goff simulates forensic situations by choosing experiment sites that are popular dumping grounds for dead bodies—unpaved service roads, vacant lots, and agricultural fields. Each experiment involves three pig carcasses that are spaced approximately 54 yards (50 meters) apart and covered with a wide screen mesh cage to prevent scavenging. The first pig is placed directly on the ground with thermocouple probes inserted

Dr. Goff examines a pig carcass suspended off the ground in order to answer questions about insect activity and time since death. (Courtesy of Dr. M. Lee Goff/Chaminade University)

to record the internal temperature of the pig as it decomposes. It is the control pig and is photographed but left untouched throughout the experiment. The second pig is set on wire mesh on the ground. Overhead, hangs a scale. Pig number 2 will be lifted and weighed each day to monitor the rate of tissue removal. The third pig is also on wire mesh and is the site for sampling insects.

For the first two weeks, the site is visited twice a day. The pigs are photographed, soil samples are taken, and weather gauges are read. A hygrothermograph measures ambient temperature and relative humidity. The rain gauge measures precipitation, and the high-low thermometer records the highest and lowest temperatures reached in a given time period.

Insects arrive at a corpse in a predictable sequence, and each new group of insects feeds on the body, making changes that attract the next group of insects. This second wave also feeds on the body, making it a

The carcass of this experimental pig is almost unidentifiable after six days of insect activity. [Courtesy of Dr. M. Lee Goff/Chaminade University]

prime feeding ground for another set of insects. Dr. Goff likens a dead body to a newly emerged volcanic island that attracts to its shores certain species of plants and animals, which take root and change the environment for future species. This orderly succession of species is the timetable on which forensic entomologists base their estimates of the time period between death and the discovery of the body. The timetables that Goff records are specific to tropical Hawaii, but there are other entomologists, such as K. C. Kim at Pennsylvania State University and Gail Anderson at Simon Fraser University in Canada, conducting similar research applicable to their climatic zones.

Insects and Death

What their research has uncovered is an intricate relationship between carrion insects and the decomposition process. Although the species vary from location to location, there are four basic categories of insects that are attracted to the various stages that a body goes through as it decays: those that feed directly on the body; those that prey on or parasitize the insects and spiders already on the body; insects that do both; and insects and spiders that use the remains as an extension of their habitat.

Shortly after death, the first wave of insects appear. These are the necrophagous species, primarily flies (Diptera) and beetles (Coleoptera) that feed directly on the body. Although evidence of decomposition is not yet visible, the flies have already honed in on the chemical changes occurring in the body. They lay their eggs in the moist cavities, such as the nose, eyes, mouth, anus, vagina, and open wounds. Because flies arrive first, they are the most precise indicators of the postmortem interval. Slower to arrive are the beetles, which prefer to feed on slightly older remains.

As decomposition progresses, the body becomes bloated as internal gases produced by putrefaction inflate the body cavity. More flies

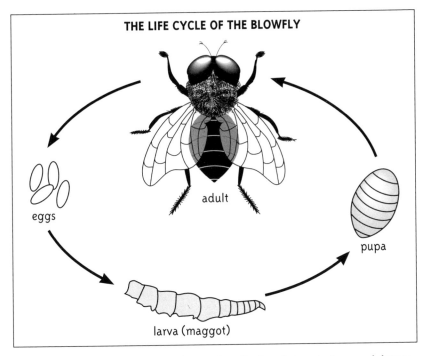

A female blowfly can lay 600 eggs in one day. The larval stage lasts several days to several weeks, after which the larva moves off to burrow into the ground, where it transforms to a pupa and then to an adult fly.

arrive, and the first maggots hatch and feed on the soft tissue. These large maggot masses can devour a corpse in a matter of days. A second group of insects, such as the burying beetles (Silphidae), rove beetles (Staphylinidae), and hister beetles (Histeridae), come to prey on the maggots. Fluid seeps into the ground, causing the population of insects normally found in the soil to evacuate, but the change in soil composition attracts other insects, some of which are microscopic. Certain wasp species (Hymenoptera) parasitize the flies by laying their eggs on or inside the maggots. When the eggs hatch, the wasp larvae feed on the tissue of the developing fly.

Wasps, ants, and some beetles feed on both the body and the other insects. Wasps will attack adult flies often on the wing, and ants will actually carry maggots off the body. There have been reports that large

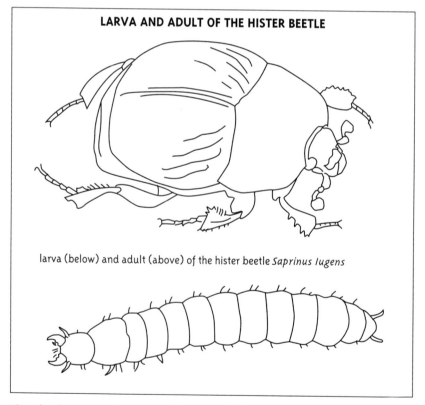

LARVA AND ADULT OF THE HISTER BEETLE

larva (below) and adult (above) of the hister beetle *Saprinus lugens*

Hister beetles prey on the eggs and maggots of blowflies found on a dead body.

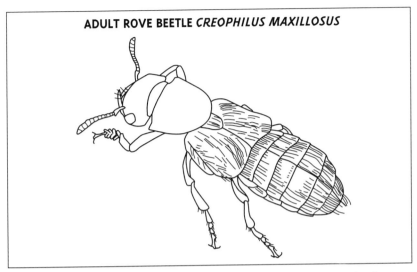

ADULT ROVE BEETLE *CREOPHILUS MAXILLOSUS*

Rove beetles arrive at a corpse after most of the flesh has been removed by decomposition and other insect activity.

ant colonies carried away so many maggots that the decomposition timetable was altered.

As the body enters the decay stage, it collapses due to the combined activities of internal decomposition and external insect feeding. The maggots that are nearing pupation wander off the corpse to find drier ground. In the post-decay stage, the body is reduced to roughly 10 percent of its original body weight. Soft tissue is almost gone, and beetles and mites dominate the scene. When only bones and hair remain, spiders can be found building webs across the skeleton. As each new species arrives and departs, they leave behind the evidence of their presence, empty egg and pupal casings as well as dung, all of which are collected for analysis.

Collecting Data

For an entomologist, it's easy to collect the proper evidence, but a forensic entomologist isn't always called to the scene. More often than not, he or she is sent mashed maggots in an envelope or asked to render an opinion based on long dead insects stored in a police evidence room. A forensic entomologist can't provide accurate information with badly handled or recorded insect evidence. To ensure that the right kind of information is collected, some entomologists have started tutoring police investigators in proper insect collection, how many to collect, and how to record the proper information that will yield a post-mortem interval estimate that would hold up in court.

Entomologist Ke Chung Kim at Pennsylvania State University takes police investigators out to the woods where they learn to collect information from one of three pig carcasses that are covered with feeding maggot masses. They are looking for representative samples of all the insects on, near, and under the body. The most important specimens are the most mature insects, because they have been on the body the longest period of time and will become the best indicators of time since death. The insects are placed in two sets of vials. One set of insects will be killed immediately to preserve or stop the biological clock. Maggots are difficult to kill because they are covered with a durable skin, or cuticle, which protects them from the elements, but entomologists have developed a fixative from a mixture of kerosene, acetic acid, and ethyl alcohol that does the job. If no fixative is avail-able, the maggots are dropped into hot water, or even hot coffee, before being transported back to the lab.

The second set of insects are kept alive to be reared in an incubat-ing chamber until adulthood. With the naked eye, all maggots look alike, and identifying larvae is difficult for even an expert, but adult insects are much easier to identify, and the length of time that the insects are in the rearing chamber lets the entomologist know when the eggs were laid.

The dead maggot specimens are identified under a dissection microscope by the shape of their breathing apparatus called posterior spiracles. The shape of the spiracles gives an indication as to what species of fly the forensic entomologist is dealing with and also how old the maggot is. Maggots grow in stages called *instars*. Their outer cuti-cle can only stretch so far before it must be shed for a larger one. In general, most flies found on corpses have three instars. An egg hatches and the first instar emerges to feed and grow until it molts into the sec-ond instar. This maggot will continue to feed until it, too, grows too large for its skin and molts into the third instar. A first instar maggot has a single pair of spiracles, the second instar has two pairs, and the third instar has three distinct sets of openings.

The third instar will stop eating and prepare to pupate. It migrates away from the body, and in some instances the migration of maggots away from the body has been so intensive that the marks left in the soil

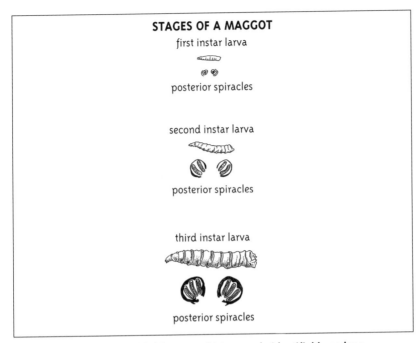

STAGES OF A MAGGOT
first instar larva

posterior spiracles

second instar larva

posterior spiracles

third instar larva

posterior spiracles

Maggots grow in stages called instars, which are only identifiable under a microscope by the shape of the posterior spiracles.

have been mistaken for tire tracks. Often times maggots reach higher ground by climbing nearby trees. Goff relates one instance at a research site where thousands of maggots were climbing the trees, crawling along the branches only to fall off the ends and start their climb all over again. So many insects were falling from the trees that the forensic entomologists needed to use umbrellas to complete their work.

Besides collecting insects, forensic entomologists collect accurate weather information for the crime scene. Insect development might be predictable and sequential, but it is also affected by temperature, and any estimate has to take into account the environmental factors associated with the time of death. Cold temperatures, for example, slow or even stop insect development, which will continue when the temperatures rise. Heat hastens insect development. The National Oceanic Atmospheric Agency (NOAA) can supply hourly or daily records of temperature, humidity levels, precipitation, and cloud cover for any of their widely scattered weather stations. Agricultural and military sources also provide weather data.

Maggot Math

The postmortem interval can be determined by the first fly's growth cycle. Researchers know how long each species cycle is under laboratory conditions and can compare that to the conditions found on the body. This is done by converting the time it takes an insect to complete its metamorphosis into Accumulated Degree Hours (ADH). For example, if a maggot is found on a corpse and is identified as a third instar of a calliphorid fly, the forensic entomologist can look back at lab studies and calculate that in controlled conditions it takes that species 45 hours to go from egg to third instar—16 hours as an egg + 18 hours as a first instar maggot + 11 hours as a second instar maggot. This is converted into ADH by multiplying the hours by the mean temperature Celsius:

45 hours × 26.7 degrees C = 1,201.5 Accumulate Degree Hours

This is changed into Accumulated Degree Days (ADD) by dividing ADH by 24 hours to get 50.0625 ADD. That is the figure that the forensic entomologist starts with to work backward through time from the moment of collection until the total number of ADH are reached.

This is done with a new set of calculations involving the mean temperature at the crime scene for each day that has passed from egg laying to insect collection. The forensic entomologist has to calculate how long that process would take under temperatures of the past few days at the crime scene.

Example:

Total ADH for the insect to reach second instar under lab conditions = 907 ADH

Day 1, October 15: A body is found and insects are collected at 9:00 A.M.
Total time elapsed = 9 hours
Mean temperature for that day = 20 degrees C
9 × 20 = 180 ADH for Day 1

Day 2, October 14:
Total time elapsed = 24 hours
Mean temperature for that day = 21 degrees C
24 × 21 = 504 ADH for Day 2

Total ADH for two days = 684 ADH. The forensic entomologist subtracts 684 from the total 907 to find that only 223.8 ADH are left unaccounted for, or less than a day's growth. To figure out what time the eggs were laid on the third day, the ADH remaining (223.8) is divided by the temperature on that day.

Day 3, October 13:

The temperature on October 13 = 20 degrees C

Divide 223.8 ADH remaining by 20 degrees to = 11.2 hours

From midnight, subtracting 11.2 hours places the time of the first insect activity to be between 12 noon and 1:00 p.m. on October 13. This is not the time of death, but the minimum time that had to have elapsed between death and collecting the insects.

Similar calculations are conducted on several species in order to get the most accurate estimate for postmortem interval. This technique of using a single insect's or species' development to determine time since death works well when the species was the first to lay its eggs on the body. But the more time that elapses between death and the discovery of the body, the less accurate the estimate will be, because several factors can alter the timetable. For example, insects are delayed from getting to exposed flesh when a body is tightly clothed or wrapped.

On New Year's Eve 1988, a body of a woman was discovered hidden in some underbrush. The body was tightly wrapped in two blankets, bound with an elastic bandage. Inside the blankets, Dr. Goff recovered several species of insects in various stages. Calculating the ADH for several of the species and taking into account the ambient temperature supplied by the weather station located a half mile away, Goff estimated the onset of insect activity at 10.5 days before the body was discovered.

Witnesses, however, claimed they had last seen the woman alive 13 days before the body was discovered. This left a gap of 2.5 days unaccounted for. To settle this discrepancy, Goff experimented on a pig carcass that he wrapped in the same manner as the victim and set out in a similar location. At the end of the experiment, Goff discovered that the first insects took precisely 2.5 days to make their way through the wrapping to get to the body and lay their eggs.

Succession Patterns

When the maggots leave a corpse, it becomes harder to determine an accurate postmortem interval, so rather than relying on fly species for an estimate, forensic entomologists determine postmortem interval by the arrival and departure of many kinds of insects over time. For example, when the body of a young man was finally discovered, most of the flies had come and gone, leaving behind a host of other insects to analyze. Goff collected a type of fly called a cheese skipper, which arrives at a corpse no later than a week after death. He also found the empty pupa of the hairy maggot blowfly that takes up to 17 days to emerge, as well as 11-day-old soldier fly maggots. Soldier flies do not come to the corpse quickly, but wait until 20 days after death to lay their eggs. Piecing together this entomological puzzle revealed an estimate of approximately 29 to 31 days of insect activity. When the police confronted the two suspects with the entomological evidence, they confessed.

Was the Body Moved?

Entomologists have known for a long time that insect species follow a very specific pattern in life, and this specificity can indicate whether a body had been moved. For example, some flies are heliophilic, which means they prefer to lay their eggs on warm surfaces or bodies sitting out in the sun. Other blowflies prefer cool temperatures and will visit only those bodies that are in the shade. There are species that prefer urban areas like the fly species *Calliphora vicina*, and those that prefer rural environments like the *Calliphora vomitoria*. If an insect is discovered on the body that is not normally from the area, then investigators can assume the corpse had been moved.

Even without a body, entomologists can tell if a corpse had once been located in a certain area by analyzing the insects that live in the soil. When a body decomposes, fluid seeps down into the ground and changes the pH levels. The insects that once were in the area leave and are replaced with insects that are attracted to the altered environment. If the postmortem interval for the soil-dwelling insects does not corroborate the postmortem interval for the insects on the body, then the police can suspect that the body had been moved after death.

Even the absence of insects can be important forensic evidence. If there are no insect larvae on a corpse that is lying outside, the police know that either death just occurred and not enough time has elapsed to attract insects, or death occurred somewhere else and the body was moved. It might also mean that the body had been frozen. Freezing a body temporarily stops decomposition, and insects will not be attracted to the remains until it has thawed.

Insects on a Suspect

Bugs on or under the body are only half the story. Bugs found on the clothes or even the car of a murder suspect could be the key evidence placing him or her at the scene of the crime. One case in Texas hinged on the single leg of a grasshopper. An exam of the body of a murdered woman revealed the remains of a mashed grasshopper. It was put aside with the other evidence, but it was not considered significant until a search of the suspect's clothing revealed a disarticulated leg of a grasshopper in the cuff of the man's pants. Microscopic analysis showed that the fracture marks on the grasshopper leg and grasshopper thorax matched.

Another case hinged on insect bites. During the recovery of a murder victim found in a field, the investigators received many nasty bites from chiggers, which are the larvae of mites. Chiggers have very specific habitat requirements and are limited to certain locations, so when one of the suspects who was brought in for questioning had similar bite marks, the investigators became suspicious. The suspect said that his welts were the result of flea bites acquired at a relative's house. The investigators set traps in and around the house to catch fleas or chiggers that might corroborate or refute the suspect's testimony, but they came up with nothing. The suspect who had prior sexual-assault arrests was linked to the body by chigger bites.

Underwater Insects

In the summer of 1989, divers exploring the murky waters of the Muskegon River in Michigan discovered a car, and when they peered through its submerged window, they saw a female body still buckled into the driver's seat. The police hauled up the car and sent the body to the morgue for an autopsy, which showed that the injuries to the woman's head were not consistent with how the car seemingly plunged into the river. Such inconsistencies usually add up to foul play, and in many cases, the police do not have to look beyond the immediate family of the victim for a murder suspect. In this case, the victim's husband was suspected of the crime.

The victim's husband claimed that he had last seen his wife in June of 1989. He told police that he and his wife had an argument and she had driven away still angry. It had been a foggy night and perhaps she had lost her way and accidentally plunged into the river. But cocoons found on the car's fender proved him to be a liar. In the winter, black flies are in their larval stage, and in the spring, they go underwater in a river or stream and weave cocoons, attaching themselves to rocks or other large hard surfaces, such as a submerged car. Because of the cocoons, the forensic entomologist determined that the car had to have been in the water no later than April or May, but not as late as June. The husband had killed his wife and dumped her car and body into the river in the spring, long before he reported her missing in June. Insects unmasked another murderer. The husband was convicted and sent to prison.

Bugs and Drugs

Because insects feed off of dead flesh, they become intimately linked with the body, capable of revealing not only the time that death may have occurred but also glimpses of how death occurred. In 1980, forensic entomologists used for the first time insect information as an alternate source for drug testing human remains.

The nearly skeletonized body of a 22-year-old woman was found near a creek bed with an empty prescription bottle at her side. Although the soft tissues had almost disappeared, there were many maggots still left on the remains. Part of the autopsy procedure for any apparent suicide would have included a drug test using the soft tissues or organs of the victim, but there was not enough soft tissue available for toxicology testing. Entomologists substituted maggots that had fed on the flesh and therefore ingested any possible drugs from the victim's tissues. Thin-layer chromatography, the same test a pathologist would use on a human liver sample, was used on the maggot material. The maggots were pureed in a blender, then placed on a glass plate and subjected to a developing solvent, which separates out the various components into visible bands. A reagent is applied to highlight the bands, revealing what kind of drug was present. When the first maggot sample was processed it revealed the presence of phenobarbital. The maggots had fed on tissue with a high concentration of the drug, corroborating the assumption that the woman died of an overdose.

Another possible overdose case involved remains that were so old they were completely skeletonized. There were no insects remaining that might have ingested soft tissue, but there were empty pupal cases and beetle droppings scattered around the skeleton. Testing hard casings had never been done before, and Wayne D. Lord at the FBI's

Forensic Science Unit Laboratory had to develop a new method, which could break down the durable chitin. The pupal cases were tested and revealed the presence of an antidepressant drug.

Because droppings and pupal cases are so durable and last many years, they offer police investigators an important tool for determining cause of death in skeletonized remains. But the recent influx of designer drugs has increased the array of possibilities in drug testing, as well as confused the assessment of the postmortem interval. More research is needed to determine the effect the drugs have on an insect's development. Entomological research is branching out in other directions too. Soon, scientists will be able to routinely extract human genetic material from bloodsucking insects like mosquitoes, lice, and bedbugs in order to trace the DNA (deoxyribonucleic acid) to the person who was bitten.

HIDDEN IDENTITY

You won't get any new ideas, really new ideas, unless you go to the collection and look at the real evidence.

—T. Dale Stewart, Smithsonian Institution

To most people, a skeleton is just a skeleton—a utilitarian structure that is designed to hold a person upright. One looks very much like another. That is certainly true for forensic anthropologists who see thousands of skeletons and can easily distinguish a tibia from a fibula, a cervical vertebra from a thoracic vertebra, or a toe bone from a finger bone. Forensic anthropologists are intimately familiar with each bone's morphology, its shape, size, curves, and construction. Yet, it is this intimate knowledge that also enables forensic anthropologists to identify an individual from mere bones, because every skeleton is different.

All humans have the same assortment of 206 bones that make up the skeletal system. But have you ever broken your arm or had a tooth pulled? Are you tall or have flat feet? Are you left-handed? All of these physical features manifest in the bone and make your skeleton unique. These skeletal markers are the nuts and bolts of the forensic anthropologist's job in determining a person's biological identity—sex, age, race, and stature. "Female, Caucasian, 40 years old, and 5 feet 1" is just a police-blotter description that could fit thousands of women, but for detectives it is the first step in identifying unknown human remains.

More specific information read from broken bones, diseases that affect the bone, deformities, and other trauma from work or sports make the description of the victim even more complete.

Living Bone

Your bones are not only a support structure but the site of red blood-cell production, mineral storage, and removal of toxins, such as arsenic and lead, from the bloodstream. Living bone is made up of a blend of compounds that gives it a unique combination of strength, hardness, and durability, as well as making it lightweight and flexible. A bone's organic collagen fibers allow it to grow, flex, and change over time, but a bone's primary components, which are inorganic compounds such as calcium, phosphorus, magnesium, and small amounts of iron, sodium, and potassium, give bone durability so that it remembers the changes it has gone through.

The process of normal bone growth and shaping is called *modeling*. It is mostly governed by genetics, but other factors, such as diet, disease, and medication, can alter the modeling process. For example, a child who is deficient in vitamin C can contract scurvy, a bone-atrophying disease. A deficiency in vitamin D results in rickets. Modeling stops when normal growth ceases around the age of 25 to 30 years of age. Bones may be fully formed, but they are still changing as they react to the stresses of injury and exercise that occur during one's lifetime. This is called *remodeling*. At the end of a lifetime of modeling and remodeling, the bones become an ossified record of a person's genetics and lifestyle.

Skeletal Collections

All of what anthropologists know about the human skeleton and its diversity is based on large documented collections made up of skeletons from morgues and university dissecting labs. The key word is documented. For each set of remains, there is a record of the person's age at death, race, sex, and stature as well as pertinent medical history. The largest of these collections is the Hamann-Todd Collection at the Cleveland Museum of Natural History that consists of more than 3,000 skeletons. The Terry Collection at the Smithsonian Institution houses 1,600 sets of remains, and the Cobb Collection at Howard University has 600. These skeletons are the research tools for anthropologists asking questions about the changes that occur in bone as a person ages, or the skeletal differences between a male and female. By carefully measuring the size, shape, and diversity of every bone, anthropologists developed standards for sexual dimorphism (differences in the shape of bone due to gender), racial characteristics, and age-related anomalies, as well as constructed mathematical formulas to estimate height from a single bone.

But these collections consist primarily of individuals who were born in the 19th and early 20th centuries, and anyone browsing through a historical fashion exhibit at a museum can see that not only fashion but the human body has changed over time. People have grown taller, and feet have gotten larger. Some anthropologists believe that using a database of older remains skews the accuracy of research and identifications. In the 1980s, Dr. Richard L. Jantz of the University of Tennessee set out to remedy any possible discrepancies by creating the Forensic Data Bank, the first modern collection to address the problems that occur when scientists try to use data from hundred-year-old remains and apply it to 21st-century murder victims. It is an ongoing collection of metric (measurable) and nonmetric (observable or descriptive) data taken from modern skeletons examined during forensic cases. This kind of collection includes a wider sampling of the population than does a military or historic collection. It includes men, women, and children of all ages and from many ethnic and socioeconomic backgrounds. Stored in boxes that look like they might hold a large bouquet of long-stemmed roses are some of the remains of the Data Bank, but the majority of the information is stored in a computer. Following standardized recording procedures, forensic anthropologists submit demographic, metric, and nonmetric observations of their forensic cases to the Data Bank, which can then be used to test new hypotheses, check if old standards still hold true, or develop new ones. Currently, the Data Bank contains information from nearly 1,400 individuals and has been used to develop FORDISC 2.0, a computer program that can be used to create specially designed ancestry and sex discriminate functions to fit specific forensic cases. The Data Bank has also revealed the new modern American skeleton.

"The amount of skeletal change since the 19th century is more remarkable than we ever dreamed it would be," Jantz said. Not only has size and stature changed, but also the shape of the bones. The skull, for example, has become narrower and higher, and the adult femur has gotten more robust and shorter. In cross section, the femur that used to be round is now teardrop shaped. Jantz suggests that the change in femur morphology may be due to decreased activity and increased height. Whatever the factors are that are affecting the change, it is clear that modern standards will lead to more accurate identifications.

Male or Female?

When forensic anthropologists are called in on a case, the first question that is asked is "Is it male or female?" The skeletal differences between the sexes are subtle and difficult to measure with a caliper and ruler. In general, the male skeleton is larger and its bones are more robust (thicker and longer), while the female's bones are more gracile, smoother, and smaller. Where muscles attach to the bone, a raised rough ridge is formed. Because males are genetically more likely to have larger muscles, they also have larger bony ridges on which those muscles are attached. These general characteristics become less distinct when looking at the vast variety of male and female shapes. The line becomes blurred comparing robust women and small-boned men, making it difficult to identify the sex of a skeleton by bone size alone.

The only functional difference between the male and female skeleton is the construction of the pelvis. The female pelvis is designed for childbirth, while the male pelvis is not, and it is estimated that if the pelvis is present at a forensic scene, a forensic anthropologist will be able to tell the sex of the victim with 95 percent accuracy.

The pelvis is made up of the sacrum and two *innominate* bones, which are also known as the os coxa. Three separate bones, the ilium, ischium, and pubis form each innominate bone, which fuse during puberty. In general, the male pelvis is narrow and deep, and the opening in the center, called the pelvic inlet—which is formed by the two pelvic halves—is heart shaped. The female pelvis is wide and shallow, and the pelvic inlet is oval to allow a baby to pass through during childbirth. On the lower edge of the ilium, the large fan-shaped bone you feel at your hip, there is a notch called the greater sciatic notch. The angle of the notch is narrow in males, less than 50 degrees. In females, the angle of the notch is greater than 50 degrees. During a quick check in the field, a forensic anthropologist can measure the notch with his or her thumb. Place the thumb in the notch: If there is room to wiggle, it is female, if it is a tight fit, it is male.

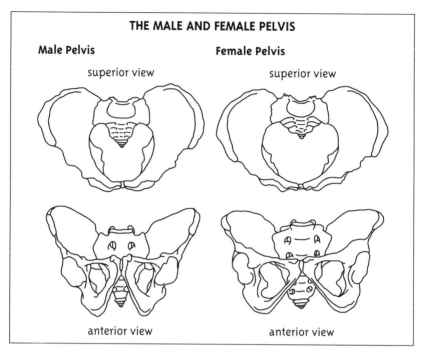

The male and female pelvis are different from each other. In general, the female pelvis is wide and shallow, and the male pelvis is narrow and deep.

At the front of the pelvis, the two innominates meet and form the *pubic symphysis*. Between them, there is a small piece of cartilage that cushions the two bones. During pregnancy, a hormone is released that softens the cartilage between the pubic symphysis so that the two bones actually separate during delivery. After delivery, the cartilage hardens again. Each softening, separation, and hardening causes pits called scars of parturition to form on the bone. By reading the extent of the scarring on the symphysis an anthropologist can tell if a woman had given birth or not.

The skull is the second most useful set of bones in the human body when it comes to determining the sex of a skeleton. During puberty, as the rest of the body is changing, the skull begins to show signs of male- or femaleness. While boys' voices are changing and their faces are sprouting hair, their facial bones become longer and more prominent. In general, males tend to have a heavier brow ridge known as the supraorbital ridge over the eyes, and the orbits, or eye sockets, are

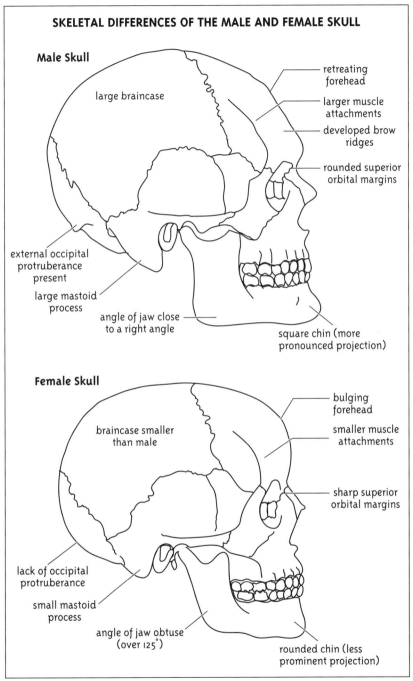

SKELETAL DIFFERENCES OF THE MALE AND FEMALE SKULL

Male Skull

large braincase

retreating forehead

larger muscle attachments

developed brow ridges

rounded superior orbital margins

external occipital protruberance present

large mastoid process

angle of jaw close to a right angle

square chin (more pronounced projection)

Female Skull

braincase smaller than male

bulging forehead

smaller muscle attachments

sharp superior orbital margins

lack of occipital protruberance

small mastoid process

angle of jaw obtuse (over 125°)

rounded chin (less prominent projection)

Skulls of men and women differ. In general, the skull of a male is larger, has more pronounced muscle markings, a heavier jaw, and a large brow ridge. The skull of a female is smaller, with fewer muscle markings and a rounded or pointed chin.

smaller and square with rounded edges. Males develop a "Dick Tracy" square chin, or mental protuberance, and a heavy mandible. On the back of the cranium, males tend to exhibit a large bump on the lower back of the head, which is a muscle attachment line called the occipital protuberance. On the side of the cranium, males have a larger zygomatic arch and mastoid process. The female skull tends to keep its gracile form—a smaller cranium, a rounded chin, and less pronounced muscle markings.

When the pelvis and skull are not present, other bones such as the bones of the arm (humerus, ulna, and radius), leg bones (femur, fibula, and tibia), and even the scapula and patella, or kneecap, can be used to indicate sex, although not as accurately. Even something as innocuous as the clavicle, or collarbone, can be used to determine a skeleton's sex. Most men have broader shoulders than women, who can have well-developed arms, legs, and back, but for the most part do not have shoulders as broad as a man's because of the clavicle, which acts as a strut pushing the shoulder out to the side. If we did not have a clavicle our arms would swing into our chests similar to the way a cow's front legs are attached to its body. The clavicle on a male is longer and extends the shoulder out farther from the body than a woman's shorter clavicle.

Because none of the methods of determining sex from a single bone, including the pelvis, are foolproof, most anthropologists agree that more than one bone should be used. New techniques are always being devised to get better accuracy, but many times the technology is too expensive to be practical in a forensic setting. The Y-chromosome fluorescence test detects the presence of the Y chromosome (the male sex chromosome) in tissue samples that have been stained with quinacrine mustard and viewed under a fluorescence microscope. The test is very accurate and can determine the sex of remains that have been dead more than 10 years. Unfortunately, it will be a long time before fluorescence microscopes become standard equipment in every police lab. In the meantime, a forensic anthropologist's skill is less expensive and just as accurate.

Age at Death

Determining how old a person was when he or she died is the second major question in the police-blotter description. The methods depend on the identification of the universal age indicators on the human skeleton that change predictably over time. We all age, but what are the changes that occur to everyone at specific times in our lives? In childhood, the changes are noticeable: The skeleton grows taller, bones thicken, teeth appear, fall out, and are replaced by adult teeth, but once a person reaches adulthood growth stops, and the changes that do occur are more due to wear and tear.

The aging process is like a roller coaster, where childhood growth and modeling of bone mass is a steep ascent followed by a leveling off and then a downward descent of bone aging and atrophy. However, the bell curve is different for everyone, because the wear and tear on the body depends on the kinds of activities a person is engaged in. A 45-year-old marathon runner, for example, will have more wear on his or her legs than a 45-year-old bookworm. Other than age and activity, nutrition, disease, and health all affect the pattern of change in the bone. Good nutrition, which includes calcium, slows the aging of bone as does skeletal stress. Studies conducted on astronauts in space demonstrated how the lack of skeletal stress due to zero gravity caused bone thinning, or osteoporosis. Inactivity causes the same condition on earth. Because of the deterioration of the bone, a skeleton of a person with osteoporosis appears older than a skeleton of the same age without the disease. In essence, anthropologists estimate biological age rather than chronological age.

To understand how the age of a skeleton is determined one has to understand how the skeleton is formed. Bones do not grow all in one unit but in pieces. For example, in the long bones of the arms and legs, the epiphyses (end caps) form separately from the shaft, or *diaphysis*, and fuse together in a process called *ossification*. The three units are held together by plates of cartilage, and each epiphysis and diaphysis has a center of ossification from which bone growth moves outward. New cartilage is formed on the outer edges as the inner cartilage is ossified to bone. In this way the bones are lengthened and eventually fused together.

At birth, a baby has some 300 separate bones, and there are 450 centers of ossification that fuse, creating the 206 bones we have as adults. You can actually see how the bones fuse by holding the bones up to a light, just like holding your hand in front of a flashlight. If there is a slight glow through the bones then they have not fully fused yet. If no light comes through, the bone is solid and completely fused.

Each bone fuses at a different and predictable rate. The two halves of the mandible at the chin's midsection are fully fused by the age of two, and the humerus, at the elbow joint, fuses together by 14 to 18

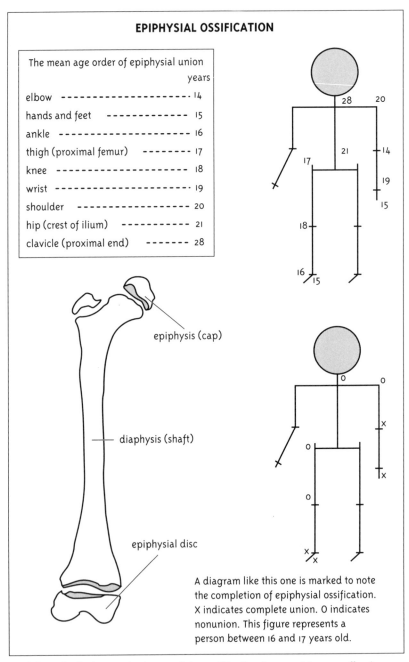

EPIPHYSIAL OSSIFICATION

The mean age order of epiphysial union

	years
elbow	14
hands and feet	15
ankle	16
thigh (proximal femur)	17
knee	18
wrist	19
shoulder	20
hip (crest of ilium)	21
clavicle (proximal end)	28

epiphysis (cap)

diaphysis (shaft)

epiphysial disc

A diagram like this one is marked to note the completion of epiphysial ossification. X indicates complete union. O indicates nonunion. This figure represents a person between 16 and 17 years old.

Each bone in the human body completes ossification by a certain age, allowing a forensic anthropologist to determine the age of a skeleton by bone growth.

years of age. The bones of the pelvis complete the growth process by the average age of 21, and the femur near the knee is ossified by 16 to 23 years of age. By the age of 24 to 30, the end of the clavicle at the center of the chest is completely fused into one bone.

The skull is also made up of 29 separate bones, which develop their own centers of ossification and gradually fuse together. An infant's skull bones are thin with a space in between to allow the head to be molded and squeezed through the birth canal. After birth, the bones begin to grow and fuse slowly, taking an entire lifetime. The squiggly lines on the skull where the bones meet are called *cranial sutures*. To determine the age of a person at death using the skull, specific segments of the sutures are assessed and given a score from 0 to 3. Zero indicates that the suture is open. One indicates that it is partially closed (less than 50 percent). A score of 2 means that it is more than 50 percent closed, and a score of 3 indicates that the suture is fully closed. The scores are added and compared to established standards. For example, a score of 11 correlates with an age range of 24 to 60 years of age with a mean age of 39.4. Because the suture method yields such a wide age range, it is best used in conjunction with another method, but in general, the metopic suture that runs down the middle of the forehead fuses by age two. The sagittal suture on the top of the head, running from front to back, fuses by age 35. The coronal suture at the front of the skull, from temple to temple, fuses by age 40.

Once all the bones are fully fused and united, the aging process begins to break bone down. They weaken, and joints form bony ridges from long years of use like the rusty buildup on old metal pipes. The pubic symphysis that is so instrumental in judging sex is also vital in judging age. As a person ages, the surface of the pubic symphysis becomes more pitted and craggy, and it can be read like a topographical map and compared with standard markers, which were first mapped out by T. Wingate Todd in 1920. The standards were later revised by T. Dale Stewart and Thomas McKern in 1957, and again in the 1980s. Dr. Judy M. Suchey at California State University examined more than 900 pubic bones of males and females autopsied in Los Angeles County from 1977 to 1979. Todd's original system of 10 phases was modified to a six-phase system and incorporated more racial variation. Determining age from the pubic symphysis is based on observation. Forensic cases are compared with plaster casts indicative of each phase. For example, a pubic symphysis of a person 20 years old would be described as billowy with noticeable ridges. As a person ages, the surface becomes more concave and the edges appear sharper.

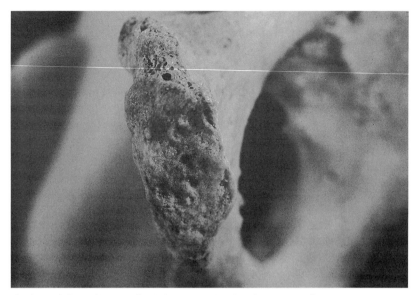

The face of the pubic symphysis becomes pitted and craggy with age.
[Kathleen O. Arries]

The one difficulty is that the scarring on the female pubic symphysis due to childbirth alters the pattern and is not the same as that found in men. Because the pelvis is subject to childbirth trauma, scientists looked for other age indicators. In the 1980s, H. Y. İşcan at Florida Atlantic University looked at a sample of 204 skeletons of known age, sex, and race and examined the end of the fourth rib where it attaches to the sternum at the center of the chest. He observed many of the same age-related changes that occur on the pubic symphysis, without the complicatins of the bone being weight bearing or involved in childbirth. İşcan mapped out the changes in the shape, size, and depth of the pits, and the condition of its margins, and categorized them over time. He observed nine phases of change covering a time span from the mid-teens to 70 years of age. Again this method is based on comparing the forensic sample with standard models to match as closely as possible all of the morphological features. In youth, the rib end is described as billowy and bulbous. Over time, the surface deteriorates and becomes hollowed out or cup shaped, and the margins become more jagged. Unfortunately, as this new standard was used and tested, forensic anthropologists discovered that considerable racial variation existed in the amount of deterioration of the end of the sternal rib. Until new standards based on race are developed, this method has limited application.

Another method for determining age at death is unfortunately destructive to the bone, and, in many cases, the anthropologist does not have permission to damage the evidence. While identifying the bodies of dead soldiers for the military, forensic anthropologist Ellis Kerley discovered a technique for telling the age of a person at death from internal bone structure. By slicing off a wafer-thin cross section of the femur or other long bone, Kerley could analyze the bone structure under the microscope. A wafer of bone as thin as one-tenth of a millimeter reveals the circular canals, or osteons, that carry blood and nourishment throughout the bone. Concentric circles form around the osteons, resembling the age rings of a tree. The older a person gets, the more fragmented the osteons become, and by comparing the number of healthy osteons to fragmented older ones, and applying them to a mathematical equation, the age at death can be calculated. It is an elaborate and time-consuming method, and although it is accurate, it is seldom used in ordinary forensic cases. It might be used in unusual circumstances, and in extraordinary archaeological finds such as the 8,000-year-old skeleton that had been preserved in a cave in Colorado. Using Kerley's method, scientists discovered that the man who crawled into the cave high in the mountains was between 35 and 40 years old when he died.

The examination of teeth, on the other hand, is readily accessible and extremely reliable, especially for determining the age of a child. The growth and development of dentition is a long, continuous, and predictable process, longer than the development of any other organ in the body. Teeth are also much less affected by environmental factors than bone and are subject to less remodeling. Because teeth are the hardest and most durable structure in the human body, they also last the longest after most bone has deteriorated.

Baby teeth, also called deciduous teeth, start to erupt at seven months and continue for the first two years. The permanent incisors and first molars erupt at 6 to 7 years, lateral incisors at 7 to 8 years, canines at 10 to 11 years, first and second premolars between 9 and 12 years, second molars at 10 to 12 years, and third molars between 17 and 25 years. After all permanent dentition has erupted, the age indicators switch from growth to wear and tear. Gum tissue is lost, and the bone underneath recedes, exposing more and more of the tooth, giving credence to the phrase "long in the tooth" as someone who had lived a long life. When determining the age of an adult, a forensic anthropologist

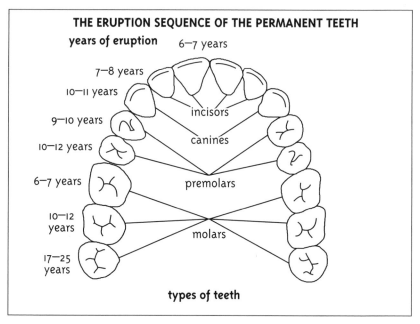

THE ERUPTION SEQUENCE OF THE PERMANENT TEETH

years of eruption   6–7 years

7–8 years

10–11 years

9–10 years

10–12 years

6–7 years

10–12 years

17–25 years

incisors

canines

premolars

molars

types of teeth

Baby teeth, or deciduous teeth, grow, fall out, and are replaced by permanent teeth at a predictable rate, making them useful age indicators.

will look at the resorption of the bone as teeth are lost, attrition, or wearing down of the tooth surface, root resorption, where the root tissue is lost, and tooth color. And in the future, perhaps looking at the rings of a tooth will yield up its owner's age. A thin layer of hard tissue called cementum forms around the root of a tooth. Each year a new layer is added and is referred to as cementum annulation, or rings of cementum. In a similar manner as Kerley's method of bone slicing, a thin cross section of a tooth root can be analyzed under a light microscope and the rings counted. Future research and a more established protocol will eventually add another tool to the anthropologist's age estimation arsenal.

Race

A person's race is more of a cultural distinction than a biological one, and the definition and determination of race has, at times, come under attack because of negative connotations and past research that was

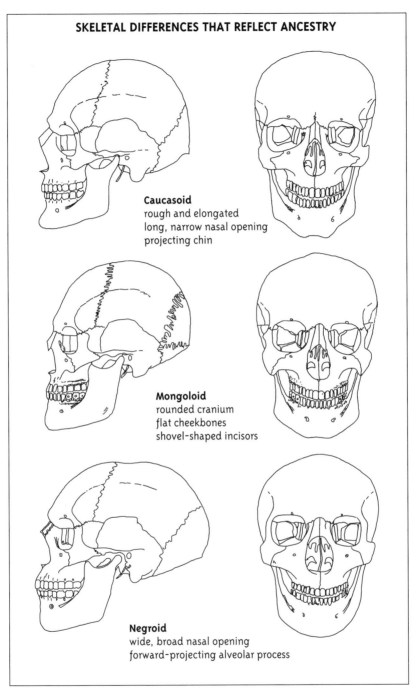

SKELETAL DIFFERENCES THAT REFLECT ANCESTRY

Caucasoid
rough and elongated
long, narrow nasal opening
projecting chin

Mongoloid
rounded cranium
flat cheekbones
shovel-shaped incisors

Negroid
wide, broad nasal opening
forward-projecting alveolar process

Anthropologists recognize three basic skeletally significant racial groups: Caucasoid, Mongoloid (which includes Asians and Native Americans), and Negroid. The most useful characteristics that reflect ancestry are found on the skull.

more political than scientific. For the forensic anthropologist, the determination of a person's racial affiliation, or ancestry, is just one more detail observed from skeletal variability that can be offered to the police so that a proper identification will eventually be made. The most useful characteristics are found in the shape of the head and face, particularly the width and length of the face, and the prognathism, or forward projection, of the bones. Although there is much cultural mixing, anthropologists recognize three basic skeletally significant racial groups: Caucasoid, Negroid, and Mongoloid (which includes Asians and Native Americans). The typical Mongoloid features include a rounded cranium, flat cheekbones and nasal opening, and shovel-shaped incisor teeth. The characteristics of the Negroid skull include a smooth and elongated cranium with a wide, broad nasal opening. The distance between the orbits is wide, and the alveolar process, the bone between the bottom of the nose and the upper teeth, projects outward.

The Caucasoid facial skeleton is rough and elongated. The nasal opening is narrow and long, and the distance between the orbits is narrow. In general, people of European descent have projecting chins. In extreme cases where the jaw extension is pronounced, it is called a Hapsburg jaw, after a recessive genetic trait of European royal families resulting from excessive inbreeding. Australian aborigines and some Pacific Islanders, however, have rounded receding chins. People of Hawaiian descent have a distinctive-shaped jaw called a rocker jaw. When the mandible is placed on the table and gently tapped, it will rock like a rocking chair because of the rounded jawbone.

Because the United States is a "melting pot," the distinctions between the races have become blurred, and many times the cultural activities that affect the skeleton indicate race better than biological indicators. In the past, some cultures have attempted to manipulate the body structure in an attempt to make it fit the culturally accepted image of beauty. Examples of this are the former Chinese practice of foot binding for upper-class Chinese females and ancient Mayan head molding that resulted in an elongated and flat forehead.

Over the years, many anthropologists have attempted to apply metric data to racial attributes to avoid the discrepancies that occur with observation alone. One method uses eight cranial measurements to derive a score that can be plotted in one of the three racial categories, and another method uses a computer program that compares specific measurements of an unknown skull to a collection of almost 2,000 individuals to find the closest racial match.

Stature

Determining the height of a person is a mathematical calculation and one of the more straightforward tasks, although the anthropologist must have already accurately determined sex, race, and age. In 1875, Thomas Dwight measured the heights of skeletons by laying out all of the bones—leg bone by leg bone, vertebrae by vertebrae, leaving tiny gaps for the tissue that fit in between. It was a tedious way to calculate the height of a person, and other scientists were determined to find an easier way. They carefully measured the bones of thousands of cadavers in documented collections and charted the relationship of individual bones to the total height of a person when they were alive. If the length of the femur was known, for example, could you figure out the total height? Could the same thing be done using the humerus or the tibia?

In 1948, Mildred Trotter along with G. C. Gleser developed a mathematical equation that could do just that. Their original work came from the accurate records of World War II dead, and then later updated with Korean War data in 1952. At the time, the only groups not fully represented were women and children, but since then more studies have been conducted and Trotter's calculations have been revised to include these groups. Trotter and Gleser's method is based on regression analysis, which is a math equation that allows you to determine an unknown measurement, such as a person's height, from several related measurements, such as the length of a leg or arm bone. The process is similar to calculating the amount of paint needed to cover a whole room based on the amount of paint used to paint one wall.

The most reliable bones to determine height are the leg bones. The femur, for example, is measured on an *osteometric board*, which looks like a large bookend with one fixed end and one movable panel. The bone is placed on the calibrated board with the lower end of the femur touching the fixed end, while the movable panel is adjusted to touch the top of the femur, just like measuring a foot at the shoe store. The measurement is read, and then plugged into a regression formula, or simply located on the appropriate Trotter-Gleser chart. For example, a black male whose femur measures 38.1 cm would have an estimated height of about 150.7 cm:

$$2.11 \text{ (femur length)} + 70.35 = \text{Stature} + \text{ or } -3.94 \text{ cm}$$

$$2.11 \,(38.1) + 70.35 = 150.7 + \text{ or } -3.94 \text{ cm}$$

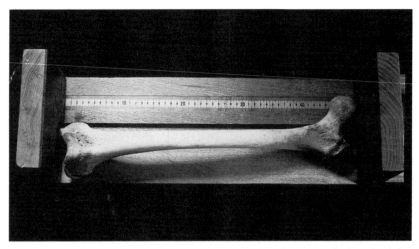

A bone is measured on an osteometric board in order to determine the length of the bone and the height of the person. [Kathleen O. Arries]

As with any estimation, the calculations are only as good as the data, and the data shows that most people misrepresent their height. On driver's licenses and other ID, women tend to underestimate their height while males tend to overestimate by as much as an inch. Even so, height estimation, like sex, age, and race, gives police enough information to start looking for a possible identification of a victim. If there is no match, the anthropologist goes back to the bones to search for more details.

POSITIVE IDENTIFICATION

. . . each skeleton is "fine tuned" to the needs of its owner and operator.

—Stanley Rhine, University of New Mexico

After determining the sex, age, race, and stature of the deceased, the next step is to look for any identifying characteristics from old injuries, diseases, and unusual features such as bowed legs, a prominent chin, or four fingers on the left hand. While forensic anthropologists examine the bones, they also collect information about the deceased through health records, medical and dental X rays, as well as interviews with relatives about the way a person walked, looked, and if he or she had ever had surgery or a broken bone. The medical data can then be compared to the skeletal data.

Antemortem details are especially important when dealing with dismembered remains, because they can provide the basis for presumptive identification. As forensic investigators prepared to identify the victims of the World Trade Center disaster, the relatives of the thousands of missing people were asked to fill out a seven-page questionnaire. What was the person's blood type? Did he have any scars? Tattoos? Did the person have a pacemaker? A lodged bullet or shrapnel? What color did she paint her toenails? Did the person have tobacco-stained teeth? What type of facial hair did he have? What size

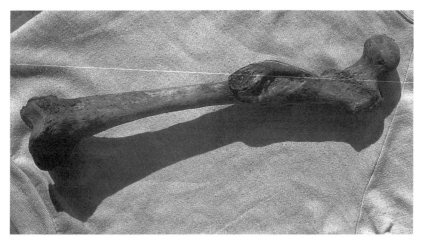

A healed fracture. Notice the bony growth at the site of the break. [Kathleen O. Arries]

wedding ring did she wear? What was the inscription? Due to the pulverizing trauma that the victims underwent, even the most minor detail could provide a clue to a person's identity.

The anthropologist also has to distinguish between trauma that occurred before death, at the time of death *(perimortem)*, or after death. *Antemortem* injuries—ones the victim survived—would help determine the person's identity, because even after a lifetime of healing, a broken bone will retain evidence of the trauma. When a bone is fractured, the area surrounding the break swells. The swelling is called a hematoma. Over time, the blood clots and a fibrous matrix, or callus, forms at the site of the break. New bone is laid down to replace the damaged area, knitting together fractured pieces, but even the most expertly set bone will retain a callus that is visible on an X ray. Bones do not have to be broken to undergo significant and recognizable changes. Our skeletons are remodeled by our work, our play, and our illnesses.

Occupational Trauma

When William Shakespeare wrote *A Midsummer Night's Dream*, he named one of the characters in the play Bottom. This amused 17th-century audiences because Bottom was a weaver, and everyone knew about the condition called "weaver's bottom." Weavers sat on hard wood floors in front of their looms all day, every day, and over the years bony growths formed on the ischium (backside of the pelvis), because of the chronic inflammation of the surrounding tissues. This painful condition made the bones bumpy and rough.

Other jobs impact the skeleton as well. Years of research has led to the identification of other physical ailments associated with particular occupations. Among them: stenographer's spread, similar to weaver's bottom, in which the pelvis gets thicker and wider; florist's fingertips, an arthritic condition that affects the bones in the fingers; and house-maid's knee, the deterioration of the knee joint from constant kneeling and bending. There is also milker's neck, which is common among farmers who milk their cows by hand, with their heads leaning against the cow's side. When the cow shifts its weight, it pushes into the farmer's neck, jamming or compressing the vertebrae in the spine.

People in many occupations and cultures throughout history have used their teeth like a tool or a third hand, leaving characteristic markings on their dentition. Electricians who use their teeth to strip wire will often have a small notch in one of their front teeth from repeating this activity over a career, and tailors and seamstresses may also have a small notch on their front teeth where they held pins in their mouth while working. Similarly, girls who used bobby pins in the 1950s would get a chip in the front tooth where they habitually slid a bobby pin into their mouth to open it before securing it in their hair. Habitual pipe smokers may have a more gradual sloping gap between the upper and lower teeth indicating where they always gripped their pipe.

In general, if you work one part of your body more than another over a long period of time, it will be reflected in the bone. The larger a muscle grows, the larger the underlying bone has to be. For example, large ridges on the femur indicate a well-developed abductor magnus muscle, which is a characteristic of horseback riders who grip the sides of the horse with their thighs. Ridges on the humerus are characteristic of someone who lifts heavy weights, such as a body builder, furniture mover, or trash collector.

It is even possible to tell if a person played a musical instrument from his or her bones. Musicians who play woodwind instruments, such as the clarinet or oboe, use the little cheek muscles to force air through the reeds of the instrument, thrusting the lower jaw forward. Doing this every day for years will produce small bumps on both sides of the mandibular condyles, the knobs that fit into the hollows of the skull, forming the hinge of the jaw. Lawrence Angel, of the Smithsonian, was able to determine that the large prominent muscle attachments on the clavicle of a dead man were evidence that he had been either a trumpet or trombone player. Angel mentioned this to the police who were able to identify the victim as a missing local musician.

Each decade brings new skeletal trauma. In the 1980s, people acquired break-dancer's knee, as well as manhole syndrome suffered by joggers who fell down open manholes. Health club groupies became inflicted with machinery knee. With repeated use, even the simplest activity can leave marks on the bone. The things we do today may become imprinted on our bones, and years from now we may have couch-potato buttocks, remote-control thumb, or Nintendo wrist.

Handedness

Being right-handed or left-handed over the years changes the appearance of the bones in the dominant arm. The ball of the humerus fits into the socket of the scapula, and with regular use the interior of the socket becomes beveled and a slight groove forms. If you are left-handed, your left shoulder socket, or glenoid fossa, will have greater beveling than your right arm. The arms of a person who plays baseball for a living or swings a hammer or throws a football will show even greater disparity. In order to compensate for the increased workload, the dominant arm will also be slightly longer by a few millimeters.

Michael Finnegan, from Kansas State University, remembered one case he worked on that tested his knowledge of handedness. Remains were brought in by the police, and judging from the skull and pelvis, they appeared to be from a female between 30 and 40 years old. Examining the skeleton for other details, Finnegan noticed that the woman had a very well-developed left deltoid process, the outer edge of the shoulder. There was a bony ridge there suggesting that she was left-handed, but the interior surface of the shoulder socket clearly indicated that she was right-handed.

The woman's tibia had large ridges where strong calf muscles would have been attached. Finnegan had seen this before in cowboys who wore high-heeled boots, and in women who wore high-heeled shoes a great deal of the time. Sometimes the shortening of the muscle is so pronounced that the person has difficulty walking in bare feet, pushing their heel down flat to the ground.

The discrepancy in the shoulder wear of the female skeleton combined with the wear of the leg bones got the anthropologist thinking about what kind of occupations could produce such skeletal markings.

Finnegan came up with the idea that the woman had been a waitress who carried large trays high over her head with her left hand and served dishes and drinks with her right hand. He also concluded that the woman probably wore high-heeled shoes as part of her work uniform. When the police identified her remains, it turned out that Finnegan had been correct—the woman had been a professional waitress.

Although approximately 90 percent of all people are right-handed, it helps tremendously to tease out the one or two left-handed people in a group of unknown skeletons. This is especially critical when dealing with a mass disaster or exhuming a communal grave.

Disease and Illness

The body of a woman remained hidden in a hastily dug shallow grave until rainwater rushing down the steep ravine exposed the left side of her skull. Just enough was visible to attract the attention of a dairy farmer out for a walk, and he called the police. The body was just 100 yards from where a psychic had taken police nine years before in an unsuccessful search for a missing woman.

When the forensic anthropologist Kathleen Arries arrived, much of the soil that had covered the body had been removed, but the dark soil-stained remains were almost indistinguishable from the surrounding earth. The skeleton was sheathed in a polyester nightgown and a fuzzy blue green bathrobe tied at the waist. The small bones of the feet were still inside dark blue socks, although some scavenging animal had pulled one sock away.

The body was removed and taken back to the police station to be examined. There, Arries determined that the woman had been in her early 20s, about 5 feet 10 inches tall, and Caucasian. She also discovered that the woman had scoliosis, an irregular curvature of the spine, and had two steel rods surgically implanted into her back. There was only one missing woman that fit that description, and she had been missing for nine years.

Scoliosis and the surgical implants provided the evidence that was needed to establish the woman's identity. X rays taken on the skeleton's spine were compared with the woman's antemortem medical X rays and were an exact match.

Anthropologists look for medical conditions that affect the bone in order to prove or substantiate identification. Most conditions, however, are not as obvious as surgical implants. Many diseases such as arthritis and osteoporosis affect the bone by stunting growth or leaving scars. Arthritis causes the cartilage to thin, and bony projections grow at the epiphyses. Osteoporosis leaves bones porous and light especially at wrists and hips.

Congenital syphilis affects the bones of the skull, radius, and ulna, and makes the tibia, or shinbone, thin and sharp. It is commonly called saber shin. There are forms of skeletal tuberculosis, which leave visible lesions on the vertebra, hip, and knee, and a disease called periostitis, which creates pitting on the bone surface.

By themselves, bone-altering diseases are good identifying markers, but some ailments offer more information like racial affiliation, occupation, or geographic location. For example, sickle-cell anemia primarily affects people of African descent, and in its severest form, it can leave scars on the bone. Thalassemia is another bone-altering form of anemia that occurs mainly in people of Mediterranean descent.

Brucellosis is a lung disease that causes lesions to form on the vertebrae. Cows carry the bacteria that causes it. The disease affects farmers, meat packers, and people who drink nonpasteurized milk. Kienbock's disease affects the hand bones of carpenters and riveters who spend long periods of time repeatedly pounding with their hands. A similar condition called carpal tunnel syndrome is common in people who work long hours typing on a computer keyboard.

Ailments specific to a particular geographic region can direct investigators to where to look for a missing person's identity. Mycetoma, for

The vertebral column of a murder victim. A cotton swab marks the groove where a steel rod had been surgically implanted in the victim's spine. (Kathleen O. Arries)

Compared to a healthy epiphysis, an arthritic joint appears rough with bony projections. [Kathleen O. Arries]

example, is a condition that affects the bones of the foot. The fungi that cause it thrive in hot and humid locations, and the condition is found primarily in people who have spent a large amount of time in the tropics.

Other kinds of diseases are contracted from the food we eat or the water we drink. Excess minerals taken in through impure drinking water are stored in the bone and can leave a person crippled or stunt his or her growth. When small pieces of bone are ground down and put through chemical analysis, they reveal concentrations of the minerals that the body absorbed over a lifetime. Some geographic areas are known to be rich in certain minerals. For example, India, Taiwan, and parts of Texas have water supplies that contain high levels of fluorine. If a body is found to have suffered from fluorosis, excessive intake of fluorine, then it may mean the person spent a great deal of time in one of those areas.

Other health problems, such as malnutrition and dental neglect, show up as eroded tooth enamel, cavities, bowing of the long bones, and signs of growth arrests, indicating that a person probably lived in poverty. A well-nourished person, on the other hand, would have well-rounded shafts of the long bones and strong teeth. Signs of extensive dental work might also indicate that a person had a certain amount of wealth.

After measuring the bones on an osteometric board, examining minute bumps under the microscope, and feeling the depth of knitting between the cranial sutures, a forensic anthropologist has to step back and look at the bones. What do all of the measurements and marks mean? Was the woman pretty? Was she healthy? Was she in need of a dentist? Did the man limp? Was he in pain? These are the types of descriptions that will help the police locate the possible identity of a John or Jane Doe. When all the pieces fit, and the bone analysis matches the information about a missing person, all that is left to do is confirm a positive identification with fingerprints, X rays, dental comparison, or DNA profiling.

Fingerprints

Pathologists routinely take a cadaver's fingerprints as part of the standard autopsy procedure, but taking the prints of a dead person can be difficult. Rather than rolling the finger over a standard fingerprint form, a device called a spoon is used, which allows a small section of fingerprint paper to be rolled over the deceased's fingers. However, during a period of full rigor mortis the hands might need to be pried open to allow the technician to apply the ink and make the print. In severe cases of rigor, the flexor tendons in the wrist might have to be severed in order to make the fingers suitably limp and maneuverable.

When there is advanced decomposition, the skin can be removed entirely and the technician's finger inserted into the skin like a second

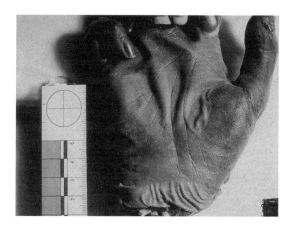

In order to fingerprint a drowning victim the technician removes the sloughed-off skin and inserts his gloved hand.
(Kathleen O. Arries)

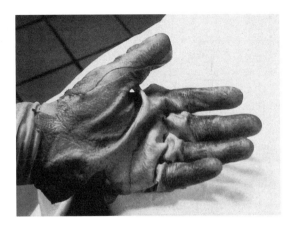

The skin on a mummified hand has to be softened with a mixture of glycol, lactic acid, and distilled water before it can be fingerprinted. (Kathleen O. Arries)

glove in order to roll the print. The skin can also be placed between two plates of glass and photographed.

Mummified or dried-out bodies can be fingerprinted only after the tissue has been softened with a mixture of glycol, lactic acid, and distilled water. The fingers are removed and may have to soak for several weeks before they are pliable enough to be fingerprinted. Mummified fingers can also be x-rayed or cast in a modeling clay or dental casting material to render a readable print.

In cases where the skin is too soft, such as occurs with a drowning victim, the prints need to be firmed up with a tissue builder. Glycerine or liquid wax is injected into the fingertip from just below the first digit. The hands of a burn victim have always been difficult if not impossible to fingerprint, but now the charred fingers can be scanned with a 3-D laser scanner to yield a digital fingerprint on a computer screen. Many medical examiners' offices do not have the skilled technicians on hand to take these kinds of prints, so the FBI offers its assistance. The FBI's Forensic Lab frequently receives mailed packages of amputated hands or fingers for fingerprinting.

The prints of a Jane or John Doe will be compared with other prints on file with law enforcement agencies like the FBI Criminal Justice Information Services (CJIS), which maintains the world's largest repository of fingerprints and receives thousands of requests a day for its services.

The classification system that the FBI uses to keep track of all those prints is a refinement of one that was first created in the 1800s by Edward Henry. It categorizes prints into eight basic patterns: plain arch, tented arch, radial loop, ulnar loop, plain whorl, central pocket whorl, double whorl, and accidental. Approximately 60 percent of all prints are categorized as some kind of loop, making it the most common type of print. Whorls, the most complicated pattern, comprise 35 percent of all fingerprints.

Each type of print is given a code, a combination of letters and numbers so that they can be easily filed and retrieved. Computer databases called Automated Fingerprint Identification Systems (AFIS) allow law enforcement agencies to compare a 10-print record against a file of half a million other records from around the country in a matter of seconds. When AFIS first went on line, many old unsolved cases were closed almost instantly. The Los Angeles police department entered fingerprints taken from the crime scenes of some 50 unsolved murders dating back more than 30 years, and the computer offered matches to many of them within minutes. In 1999, the FBI installed

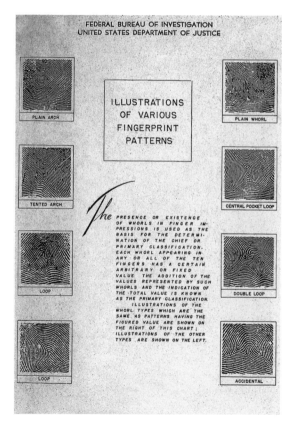

Fingerprints are classified based on eight basic patterns first identified by Edward Henry in the 1800s. [Kathleen O. Arries]

an improved system called the Integrated AFIS (IAFIS) that can be linked with a system of police-car scanners, allowing a police officer to fingerprint a suspect or victim at the scene, scan in the live prints, and compare them against the database of some 34 million digitized FBI print cards. This would prevent those near misses that occasionally plague police officers who pick up a person on a minor infraction and later find that he or she is wanted for a more serious crime. At a car terminal, or typically at a police station or medical examiner's lab, fingerprints are scanned into the machine, and the computer program converts the image into a spatial map and then into digital binary data. As each print is scanned, it is compared with prints already in the system. IAFIS can match an unknown print with one on file with 98 to 100 percent accuracy.

But the computer system is only as good as the people who use it, and not all police departments have the facilities to adequately use the system. Contrary to popular belief, not everyone who is arrested is fingerprinted, nor are all fingerprints filed with the FBI. For example, if the police in Buffalo, New York, fingerprint someone, they may or may not send the file on to CJIS. The more severe the crime, the more likely the records will be forwarded. Difficulties arise, too, with small precincts. Approximately 50 percent of all police forces have 10 officers or less, and 20 percent have only one officer.

The IAFIS computer program uses a scoring system that assigns prints to each of the criteria set by the operator. Although IAFIS has the capabilities to search for "cold hits," matching a latent print with an unknown suspect already in the computer, it is more likely that a computer operator would enter in a set of criteria. For example, the medical examiner with a Jane Doe might enter "white female, 5 feet 10 inches tall, mid-40s," and the computer would search in those parameters and select the closest correlations.

Although everyone has a unique set of fingerprints, it is possible to find two people with the same preliminary classification code. In theory, two people could have the same fingerprint classification code if both have thumbs that are loops, index fingers that are tented arches, middle fingers that are whorls, etc. The computer would select those people along with perhaps eight or nine other close correlations, which would then be scrutinized by an expert who would look at the tiny ridge characteristics or minutiae that make one person's print different from another. Minutiae include any ridge endings or bifurcations (the branching out of one ridge into two), ridge dots, enclosures, short ridges, and bridges and trifurcations. It is this attention to detail that catches a killer or identifies his victim. Although there are no hard-and-fast rules as to how many points of similarity are required to call two prints matching, the rule of thumb is approximately 12. No expert would declare a match with less than eight points of similarity.

Using fingerprints to identify the deceased means little if the person does not have his or her prints on file. In these instances, the forensic anthropologist's police-blotter description will hopefully render a list of possible suspects. Latent fingerprints can then be lifted from the homes and personal effects of those suspects and used for comparison. After the Oklahoma City bombing, 19 children were identified using the latent prints lifted off of the television screens they had touched while watching TV in their homes.

Sinus Prints

If a body is so badly decomposed that it cannot be identified visually, then chances are the fingerprints are unreadable also. There are other kinds of prints that can be used, such as sinus cavity prints. On an X ray, a person's sinus cavity shows a scallop-shaped pattern at the top edge. Sinus prints were used in 1978 by a team of forensic scientists appointed by a congressional committee to review the medical data surrounding the assassination of John F. Kennedy. Rumors of a body-switching conspiracy had spread, and a forensic team used X rays of Kennedy's sinuses before and after death to conclude that the remains were indeed of Kennedy and not someone else.

Forensic Odontology

Not everyone has had their sinuses x-rayed, but most people do have their teeth x-rayed at the dentist's office, and like sinuses, teeth are unique identifying features. Unlike the delicate bones lining breathing passages, tooth enamel is hard and durable, withstanding most kinds of trauma such as fire or crushing blows that would otherwise destroy skeletal evidence. Scientists who specialize in comparing and matching dental X rays with skeletal X rays are called forensic dentists, or odontologists, and they frequently work in conjunction with forensic anthropologists to confirm the identification made from the skeletal data.

The most common form of dental ID is based on the comparison of the postmortem dentition with antemortem dental records, which may include X rays, dental casts, and written examination notes. This requires that the investigators have some idea of the identity of the remains. Typically a wallet or other information found near or on the body will give the police a tentative ID, or a forensic anthropologist will supply a skeletal description of the person. This is usually enough to locate and request antemortem dental records.

First, the *forensic odontologist* examines the dental remains to chart and make detailed recordings of all anomalies and points of possible comparison. An adult has 32 teeth, each with five surfaces giving a forensic odontologist 160 surfaces that can be visually examined. X rays taken of the dentition and jaw offer further points for the comparison of root shape and tooth eruption. The more dental or restorative work a person has had, the more points of comparison there are and therefore an increased chance of determining identity. But there is no minimum number of features required to make a positive ID. A single tooth may yield identity as long as it has sufficiently unique characteristics. Conversely, a mouthful of teeth may lack enough distinct features for comparison.

After the postmortem X rays are taken and visual exam is completed, the remains are compared with antemortem records. Do they have similarly shaped fillings and restorative work? Is the eruption sequence similar? All discrepancies are noted. Some differences may be explainable. For example, a tooth that is missing or diseases that have progressed may be attributed to the length of time that has elapsed since the date of the last antemortem dental visit. Any unexplained discrepancies, such as a tooth that is present at the postmortem exam but is absent on the antemortem records, would be cause for exclusion.

Forensic odontologists will declare a positive ID if a sufficient amount of the dentition matched the antemortem record with no unexplained discrepancies. A possible ID means that the remains have consistent features with the antemortem record, but the quality of the evidence or the antemortem record is insufficient to warrant a positive ID. Dentition that is clearly inconsistent with the antemortem record will be excluded. Additional records must be found and the process repeated.

Other means of identification can be made by fitting dentures to casts kept by dentists or identifying unusual dental materials. The latter can be tracked down to where the restorative work may have been performed or the geographic region where the work is commonly practiced. The earliest case of denture ID may have been made by Paul Revere in the 1770s. Although known for his copper and silver work, Revere also practiced dentistry. He often made false teeth like the set he made for his friend Dr. Joseph Warren. The teeth were held together by silver wire and supported by a bridge made from a hippopotamus tusk. Years later, General Warren was shot in the head and died at the Battle of Bunker Hill on June 17, 1775. His body was unceremoniously buried in a mass grave. Warren's family wished to take him back to England, and Revere was able to identify his body from all the rest based on the dental remains.

If there are no clues as to the location of antemortem records or none exist for comparison, then forensic dentists can help police limit the list of possible suspects with a postmortem dental profile. This corresponds to the forensic anthropologist's police-blotter description and includes age, ancestry, sex, socioeconomic status, habitual behaviors, and other characteristics.

Race may be determined by careful examination of the cusps of the molars and shape of the incisors. Caucasians exhibit an extra cusp on the maxillary first molar, which is often called Carabelli's cusp. Native Americans have shovel-shaped incisors compared to Caucasian or Negroid blade-shaped incisors.

The eruption of the deciduous, or baby, teeth and the wear of the permanent dentition can determine a person's age. There are no dental distinctions between male and female teeth, so forensic dentists, like anthropologists, refer to the size and shape of the skull.

Teeth also reveal other aspects or habits of a person. Stains on the teeth are common among smokers or might indicate that the person used the antibiotic tetracycline when the teeth were developing. Erosion on the interior surface of the teeth may indicate the person suffered from repeat vomiting caused by an eating disorder, chronic gastrointestinal problems, or alcoholism.

The Dentists of DMORT

Forensic odontologists are particularly important at mass disaster sites. When DMORT was activated after September 11, more than 100 dentists left their practices and traveled to New York City to work with Dr. Jeffrey Burkes, the chief forensic dentist for the New York City Medical Examiner's office. They worked four- to six-hour shifts, rotating through four stations. The "Go Team" was sent to the site to retrieve dental evidence and safeguard their transport back to the morgue. The antemortem team transposed and entered into the computer the dental records brought in by the families of those who were missing. Because of the massive amount of information, the records were entered into two different computer programs to protect against a power failure. "It is a staggering task," Dr. Burkes said. "Without computers we would be lost."

The postmortem team, consisting of three dentists, spent their shift examining the remains. One dentist would call out dental structures, while a second dentist cleaned the remains and double-checked the first investigator's observations. The third forensic odontologist recorded the information.

The comparison team looked at both the antemortem records and postmortem exams to find a match and, therefore, the identity of a victim. When no positive identity was ascertainable, then a sample of pulp from the interior of a tooth or a bit of muscle tissue was sent to a lab for genetic testing.

IT'S IN THE GENES

Basic science. It leads us in unexpected directions that have social consequences.

—Dr. Eric Lander, MIT Center for Genome Research

A tiny bit of pulp from the interior of a tooth, a small vial of blood, a sample of bone, or a swab of saliva is all forensic biologists need to discover a person's identity. They don't need to see every tooth or every bone to be able to create a personal printout of your genetic code.

Inside the nucleus of almost every living cell is *DNA* (deoxyribonucleic acid), the building block for every living thing. It carries the genetic information that determines what every cell in the body will be and how it will function. It determines whether an animal becomes a mammal or an amphibian, or whether a person has blue eyes or brown hair.

DNA is shaped in a double helix, a spiral staircase of chemical bonds. If uncoiled, the DNA looks more like a ladder; a long string of simple repeating units. Each side consists of long strands of nucleotides consisting of a phosphate, a sugar, and one of four bases: adenine (A), cytosine (C), guanine (G), and thymine (T), which bond to form the rungs of the ladder. But A only pairs with T, and G only pairs with C. A base sequence of A-G-T-C will only bond with a strand sequence of T-C-A-G. It is this simple pairing that forms the many variations between species and between individuals in a species.

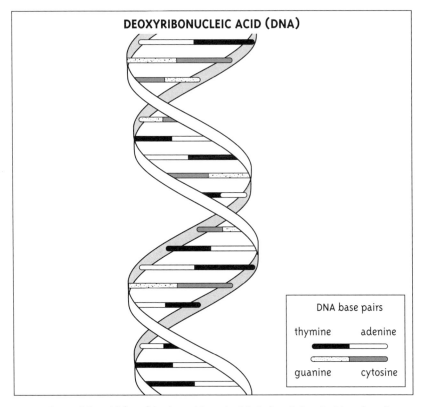

DEOXYRIBONUCLEIC ACID (DNA)

DNA base pairs

thymine   adenine

guanine   cytosine

Deoxyribonucleic acid (DNA) is shaped in a double helix of chemical bonds—a long string of simple repeating units. The four bases that make up the molecule are adenine (A), cytosine (C), guanine (G), and thymine (T).

Specific segments of DNA that control the production of proteins are called genes. The entire human genetic code, or genome, consists of 80,000 to 100,000 genes and about 3 billion nucleotide letters. This mass of information is organized and bundled in threadlike packages called chromosomes. Humans have 23 pairs of chromosomes, receiving one-half from each parent. Because all humans have one head, two arms, two legs, and breathe, eat, and think in the same manner, most of the genetic code is the same for everyone. For example, the sequence that codes for humans having ten fingers is the same for all primates. But the sequence that codes for the size and shape of those fingers is different for each species. Within the human genome, there is only a small amount of genetic material, about 0.01 percent that is different.

It seems like an insignificant amount, but that small percentage amounts to 3 million rungs on the ladder that vary from person to person, giving us our own unique characteristics. These differences are called polymorphic segments, or hypervariable regions, which are scattered throughout the genome. They also hold the clue to determining a person's identity.

In a Leicester Lab

In 1984, Dr. Alec Jeffreys was working with DNA at the Lister Institute of the University of Leicester in England. His goal was to find ways to map DNA in order to study it better. What he discovered was a way to reveal a person's unique DNA structure. Jeffreys used radioactive markers to locate hypervariable regions, which were then separated out and exposed on radiographic film. What resulted was a series of fuzzy black bands that resembled a grocery product's bar code. Just as a bar code identifies a specific product, the dark bands showed the DNA arrangement that is unique for each individual. He also discovered that the pattern would be the same whether the DNA sample came from saliva, tissue, blood, hair follicles, urine, semen, or bone.

The First DNA Manhunt

In 1983, less than 10 miles from the Leicester Lab, a 15-year-old girl named Lynda Mann was raped and murdered along a footpath in the village of Narborough. Three years later, another 15-year-old girl, Dawn Ashworth from the nearby town of Enderby, was brutally attacked and killed in a similar secluded area. The murders occurred three years apart, but the police were convinced that the same person committed both crimes. There were no fingerprints and no eyewitnesses, and the only physical evidence was the rapist's semen found on the girls' clothing. The police suspected a young man named George Howard, who had several prior minor sex offenses and who had been seen near the crime scene the night Dawn Ashworth had been killed. During grueling interrogations, the confused Howard confessed to killing Dawn Ashworth but insisted he did not know anything about the death of Lynda Mann.

A forced confession was not enough to ensure a conviction. What the police really needed was to prove that the semen samples came from Howard. Although DNA testing had never been applied to forensic work before, the police contacted Jeffreys and asked for his help. Jeffreys tested the two semen samples, as well as Howard's blood, and came up with three DNA fingerprints. Two were identical, but the third was completely different. The semen samples yielded identical DNA fingerprints, but neither matched Howard's blood sample. The police were right in suspecting the same person killed both girls, but that person was not George Howard. He had given a false confession and was exonerated by his own DNA. It was the first case where DNA proved a suspect's innocence.

In January 1987, armed with only one DNA fingerprint profile, the police launched the first DNA manhunt. They intended to test the blood of every man in the towns of Narborough, Enderby, and Littlethorpe, and places in between. They could not force anyone to participate, but men aged 17 to 34 were asked to submit to the test as part of their civic duty to catch a killer. Testing centers were set up at hospitals and doctors' offices, and mobile units patrolled the countryside.

After eight months of testing more than 4,500 men, the police were still without a DNA match. But in September 1987, a policeman whose father owned a pub heard about several bakery workers discussing how fellow coworker Colin Pitchfork had paid someone to impersonate him and give a blood sample. Police searched through the blood tests and discovered that Colin Pitchfork's signature on the release form did not match those on other official documents. Pitchfork was brought in for questioning and asked to submit a blood sample. When it was tested, Pitchfork's DNA fingerprint matched the two samples taken from the murdered girls' clothing. This case became the first conviction based on DNA evidence.

DNA Profiling

Today the process of DNA fingerprinting, or profiling, is a refinement of Jeffreys's original method. No matter what the sample is, blood, tissue, semen, vaginal fluid, teeth, hair, or bone, the DNA must be extracted from the cells. This is done by dissolving the cell walls with a chemical detergent, which releases the DNA from its nuclear and chromosomal packaging. The DNA is then tested to determine its quality and quantity. If there is a large amount of high quality DNA present, then Jeffreys's method, called Restriction Fragment Length Polymorphism (RFLP), is used.

MAKING A DNA PRINT

1) DNA is extracted from a cell's nucleus.

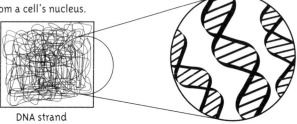

DNA strand

2) It is dissolved in a solution of enzymes that target specific points on the DNA, cutting the strand into smaller fragments.

3) A small amount of DNA is then placed in a tray of special gel. An electrical current is sent through the gel, pulling the fragments along and arranging them by length and weight. The smaller fragments are pulled the farthest to the other side of the tray, while the larger, heavier fragments come to rest sooner.

suspect's DNA fragments

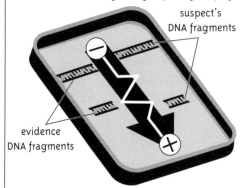

evidence DNA fragments

4) The fragments are then transferred to a nylon membrane where a radioactive probe is applied. X-ray film is placed over the membrane for several days. The probes seek out and mark specific points on the DNA, creating dark bands to appear on the X-ray film. The film becomes the DNA print, which can then be compared to other prints until a match is found.

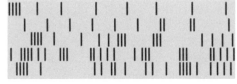

Everyone has a unique set of DNA and, therefore, a unique DNA profile. But the process only maps a small percentage of the total DNA, so there is a slight chance—one in several million—that another person might have the same profile.

The DNA strands are cut into pieces using restriction enzymes. For example, a commonly used enzyme called Hae III cuts DNA everywhere the bases are arranged in a GGCC sequence. The length of these DNA segments are measured to see how many times the specific DNA segment is repeated. The size varies for each person. They may be as small as a few hundred base pairs or as large as 10,000.

The segments are then separated by electrophoresis. The DNA fragments are loaded into a well at the base of a slab of gel. An electrical current is applied, which forces the negatively charged DNA to move toward the positively charged electrode at the other end of the gel. The smaller fragments move faster and farther than the larger particles, so that a fragment's location on the gel is determined by its length or molecular weight.

The DNA is then stained so it can be seen under ultraviolet light and chemically separated into its single-stranded form. Then a sheet of nylon is placed over the gel, and the DNA is lifted off in what is called a Southern blot.

The DNA on the blot is then subjected to DNA probes, which are radioactive single-strand DNA sequences that act as guided missiles to travel down the DNA fragments and seek out complimentary base pairs. When they find a match, the strands connect. The excess probes are washed away, and the blot is placed on a sheet of film and exposed to a radioactive tracer and developed into an autoradiograph, or autorad. The autorad is what looks like a grocery product's bar code.

RFLP works well when the sample that is being tested is large and of high quality, but DNA degrades rapidly during the decomposition process or when exposed to heat. Frequently, the samples are too fragmented to be useful. In the 1980s, a process called polymerase chain reaction (PCR) was developed that takes degraded or small quantities of DNA and amplifies them. As little as 2 nanograms (2 billionths of a gram) is required compared to 20 to 50 nanograms of DNA that is required for RFLP. Today, saliva from a piece of chewed gum or a licked stamp is enough for testing. In Australia, scientists have even been able to obtain a DNA profile from touched objects. Researchers swabbed briefcase handles, telephone receivers, and pens and managed to get DNA profiles for anyone who recently touched the object.

PCR searches for short segments, called short tandem repeats (STRs), that are repeated in the DNA. These are separated out and amplified using a process similar to DNA's natural replicating process during cell division. PCR can replicate these segments a million times in about one hour. This larger amount is then processed to reveal the telltale DNA pattern. Four or more searches of different segments are usually done to limit the chances that the same person would have a similar code. The chances of that happening has been estimated at one in several million. The FBI forensic standard is to analyze 13 sites.

CODIS

Forensic genetic information is now processed on a computer to yield a digital code that consists of 50 to 70 numbers and can be stored in a database like the FBI's Combined DNA Index System (CODIS). Initiated as a pilot project in 1990, CODIS links state and local forensic laboratories so that they can store and access DNA profiles of convicted offenders, missing persons, and from unsolved crime scenes. All DNA profiles entered into the system are automatically checked against those already in the system. Since its installation, CODIS has assisted in more than 1,900 investigations in 31 states, linking crime scenes and identifying serial killers and rapists. In 1999, two female college students were sexually assaulted but unable to positively identify the offender. Circumstantial evidence and witness descriptions led police to a suspect. The man's DNA was tested and entered into the database. CODIS automatically ran the DNA code through both the Convicted Offender Index and the Forensic Evidence Index and came up with a match. The suspect's DNA was linked to three other sexual-assault cases that occurred in 1994 and 1995.

In 1998, the FBI installed the National DNA Identification Index (NDIS), creating a vital link between more than 100 labs in more than 35 states. To date, all 50 states have passed laws requiring DNA testing of sexual offenders, more than half have laws including felons convicted of violent offenses such as murder, manslaughter, arson, kidnapping, and robbery, and 10 states have enacted legislation to include all felons. With this much information, there is a backlog in testing and filing DNA profiles, but the FBI currently holds more than 600,000 DNA profiles from convicted criminals and more than 26,000 forensic samples. The FBI's Missing Persons Index is much smaller, but it does include nuclear DNA profiles of missing persons, unidentified murder victims, and body parts, as well as profiles made from a second type of DNA.

From Mother to Child

Your cells actually contain two kinds of DNA, nuclear DNA that is found in the nucleus of the cell and *mitochondrial DNA* (mtDNA) that is found in an organelle called a mitochondria. Mitochondrial DNA contains only one set of DNA inherited through maternal lines. The female's mtDNA is contained in the egg, but the male's mtDNA is found in the tail of the sperm. At the moment of fertilization, the sperm head enters the egg, but the tail detaches and the male's mtDNA is lost to the next generation.

Using mtDNA for profiling has some advantages. For example, scientists have discovered that mtDNA is more abundant than nuclear DNA. There might be several hundred mtDNA molecules per cell, yielding a greater likelihood of success in the testing process. Mitochondrial DNA also does not degrade as quickly as nuclear DNA and can last thousands of years. Scientists recently found and tested the mtDNA of the skeletal remains of a Neanderthal estimated to be 40,000 to 50,000 years old. And because mtDNA is inherited only through the maternal line, it does not change. It is passed down in virtually identical form from generation to generation. Scientists estimate that mtDNA changes only once every three to four thousand years.

In 1997, mtDNA was extracted from a tooth of a 9,000-year-old skeleton known as Cheddar Man, a Stone Age hunter-gatherer discovered in an underground cave in Cheddar, England. In an unusual experiment, the ancient mtDNA was compared with mtDNA of living residents of Cheddar and miraculously found a match. A history teacher named Adrian Targett shared a common maternal ancestor with Cheddar Man more than 10,000 years ago.

Mitochondrial DNA's ability to last unchanged for years makes it uniquely qualified for use in forensic situations involving skeletal material. The physical evidence is often fragmentary and in an advanced stage of decomposition. There is usually little or no nuclear DNA remaining intact. In these situations, mtDNA may be the only available form for testing. Although forensic anthropologists do not perform DNA profiles, they do deal with cases, such as missing persons, that may ultimately be resolved using DNA analysis. The role of the forensic anthropologist in these situations is to help narrow down the field of suspects. Mitochondrial DNA is only useful when there is another subject to compare it to. A forensic anthropologist working with skeletal remains may be asked to supply samples to the

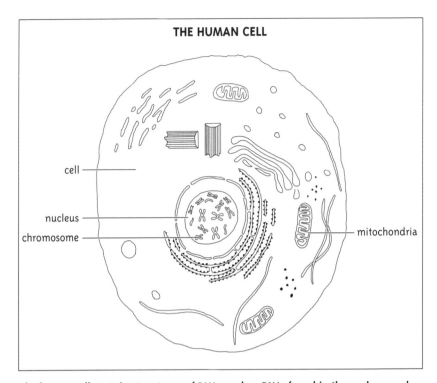

THE HUMAN CELL

cell
nucleus
chromosome
mitochondria

The human cell contains two types of DNA: nuclear DNA, found in the nucleus, and mitochondrial DNA, found outside the nucleus in the organelles called mitochondria. Nuclear DNA is inherited from both parents, while mtDNA is inherited only through the maternal line.

FBI Lab, which requires at least 3 to 5 inches of long bone or several teeth, in particular, the molars and premolars that are free of dental restoration.

The resulting profile is compared with profiles made from a likely suspect's personal effects: the hair from a brush, blood from a crime scene, or even a medical biopsy sample. But most often they are compared to the mtDNA profiles of a next of kin—a sibling, mother, or other relative related through the maternal side of the family.

Millions of Tests

No one would have realized just how necessary DNA testing would be until September 11, 2001. Right away, the forensic community knew that the normal avenues of identification—fingerprinting, dental records, and X-ray comparison—would not be sufficient because of the cremating heat and pulverizing forces that acted on the bodies as the twin towers fell. DNA testing had never been done on such a massive scale before. It was used for the first time to identify the victims of an aviation accident in 1996 after the crash of TWA Flight 800 off of Long Island. The process took a year to complete, but 22 of the 230 people on board would not have been identified without it. It then became standard procedure after a plane crash. The Armed Forces Institute of Pathology performed DNA tests for the passengers and crew aboard United Flight 93, as well as those aboard American Flight 77, which struck the Pentagon. The military personnel who died on the ground at the Pentagon were readily identified by DNA, because the military retained blood samples of all of their servicemen and servicewomen. However, the identification process following the World Trade Center disaster proved to be 20 times more massive.

The day after the tragedy, a line of parents, siblings, husbands, and wives stretched two blocks around the Family Crisis Center set up at the 69th Regiment Armory. They filled out a seven-page missing person's report. Many carried a toothbrush or hairbrush in a Ziploc bag. Mothers, brothers, and sisters submitted their own DNA—saliva swabbed from the inside of their cheeks—for testing.

Although the New York City medical examiner's office had the largest forensic DNA facility in the country, it could never handle the volume that was expected to come, especially after officials pledged to test every piece of tissue found. That meant the possibility of testing the same person several times, but the city was committed to identifying all remains, if possible. Two genetic testing labs were contracted to handle the overflow. If families provided direct samples of a victim's DNA from an unwashed garment, toothbrush, biopsy sample, or strand of hair, then a direct nuclear match would be attempted by Myriad Genetics in Salt Lake City, Utah. When no direct samples were available, cheek swabs taken from relatives were sent to Celera Genomics in Rockville, Maryland, to be tested for mtDNA.

Using an automated system, the New York City lab could extract DNA from as many as 4,000 tissue samples a day. Time was a factor. It was important to be able to recover body parts quickly before the DNA began to degrade. Once the body parts were recovered, they could be refrigerated until tests could be run. By November 2001, when the first identifications using DNA were made, eight families were notified that the remains of their loved ones had finally been found.

11

CAUSE OF DEATH

It is easy to reconstruct events from evidence of damage to the skeletal remains, but it is very difficult to do so correctly.

—William Maples, C. A. Pound Human Identification Laboratory

When police presented forensic anthropologist Michael Finnegan with a skull that appeared to have a bullet hole, they wanted to know what caliber bullet was responsible. Finnegan measured the hole and suggested that it might have been a .25. That caliber bullet would be rather rare these days, and an officer asked if Finnegan meant a .22, which would seem more likely. But Finnegan held firm. It was definitely a .25, and he could also name the model of the weapon—a Black & Decker. Thoroughly confused, the officer questioned Finnegan again.

"You mean a Smith & Wesson?"

"No." Finnegan said. "A Black & Decker. It's a drill hole."

As it turned out, the old skull had been a morbid tavern decoration and had been drilled a long time ago to add to its mystery.

Forensic anthropologists know their tools, and deciphering what kind of injury results from a particular tool or instrument is one of the most gruesome aspects of forensic anthropology because it relates so directly to the mind-set of the murderer and the pain of the victim. But

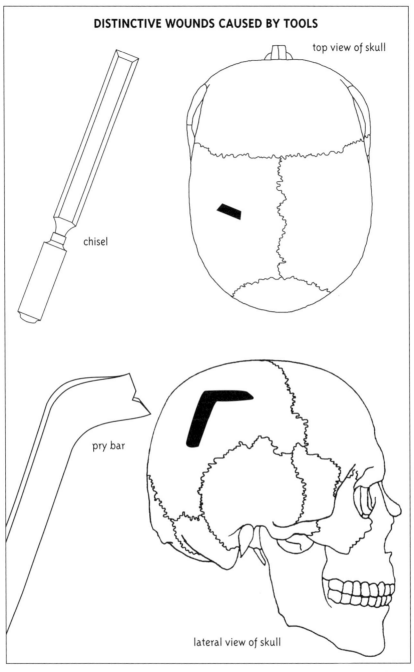

DISTINCTIVE WOUNDS CAUSED BY TOOLS

top view of skull

chisel

pry bar

lateral view of skull

Tools used as weapons leave distinct wounds. The perforation in the left side of the skull (see top image) was caused by a chisel as it passed through the bone. The shape of this injury corresponds precisely with the angle and shape of a pry bar (see bottom image).

analyzing and interpreting violent trauma was not originally part of a forensic anthropologist's job description. Forty years ago, W. M. Krogman wrote: "I don't think the physical anthropologist should tackle cause of death. This sort of thing . . . is ably handled in any good text in pathology or in forensic medicine." The difficulty with this attitude is that most signs of trauma are lost when flesh decomposes, and pathologists are not the most qualified to collect and interpret skeletal data.

Twenty years later, T. D. Stewart broached the subject again and provided the science with a definitive stance when he wrote: "For this reason a forensic anthropologist should simply describe any evidence of bone damage, point out its location in relation to vital centers, explain the possibility of its having been sustained at the time of death or otherwise, and discuss the likely types of objects that produced the damage."

Frequently what happened at the time of death is not clearly apparent, and in these instances, forensic anthropologists try to recreate the particular trauma in order to match the unknown injuries to the known. "All skeletal interpretation can be difficult," Douglas Ubelaker says. "A lot of these cases take us to the edge of our knowledge. My approach has always been that we have to be creative and responsive to the problems that are presented to us, and sometimes if we don't have the knowledge immediately we can find the knowledge in the collection of 33,000 skeletons at the Smithsonian Institution or through experimentation."

Every forensic anthropologist experiments with various kinds of tools and weapons. According to the *Forensic Anthropology Training Manual* by Karen Ramey Burns: "The student will benefit by experimenting with fresh bones obtained from a local butcher. Examine the marks made by every tool available."

Chicken Legs and Finger Bones

A classic case of experimentation involved a case Dr. Ubelaker worked on involving a Puerto Rican girl who had been found murdered and left in a Virginia berry patch. Ubelaker's predecessor at the Smithsonian, Larry Angel, had worked on the case and noted that one of the girl's fingers had been cut off. The police had no other leads, and the girl's body was returned to Puerto Rico for burial. As if knowing that it would be needed someday, Angel packed the bones and placed the finger bone in a small plastic bag and labeled it.

Years later, new evidence was uncovered by police. Larry Angel had died, so Ubelaker made the trip to Puerto Rico to exhume the body. In the small coffin he found Angel's note along with the finger bone in the plastic bag. Angel had not known what caused the trauma, and now it was up to Ubelaker to find out.

The bone had a straight, almost clean cut at one end. It did not have the parallel cut marks of a knife, and it did not have the gnawing marks of a rodent, but nothing could be ruled out just yet. What had caused the finger to be cleanly cut like that?

Inspired by the supermarket display of chicken legs that he was buying for a Memorial Day picnic, Ubelaker decided to experiment. Chicken bones are different from human bones. Animal bones are denser, but the leg of a chicken and the finger of a human are close in size and thickness and in a purely experimental setting may give some clues about the type of trauma that occurred.

With the raw skin and meat still on the bone, Ubelaker sliced one chicken leg with a sharp kitchen knife and another with a dull kitchen knife. He chopped another in half with a machete and another with a large flat pickax called a mattock. Three more bones, held in place and not held in place, were slammed in a car door. The last chicken leg was run over with the lawn mower, which is a common occurrence for bodies that have been dumped along the roadside in tall grass.

Each fractured chicken leg was labeled and set in boiling water to cook all the meat away. After the bones were cleaned, Ubelaker examined the kinds of trauma that resulted. The knife cuts showed the shape of the edge of the knife blade, and the bone that was run over with the mower was completely destroyed. The trauma left by the mattock and the car door seemed similar to that of the girl's finger bone. However, since there was no other trauma on the skeleton that would suggest that the killer bludgeoned the victim, it seemed to make sense that at the time of death, the girl's finger had been cut off in the killer's car door.

Ubelaker's experiment did not provide enough evidence for the prosecution. The attorneys needed to know if the experiment would work with a 1974 Ford Pinto, which was the make and model of the car driven by the suspect. Ubelaker and the police located a citizen willing to have a chicken leg slammed in the door of his 1974 Pinto. They conducted another 18 experiments. Only one experiment produced the clean sheared-off cut similar to the one on the victim's finger. It seemed quite possible that the finger had been cut off in a car door. The suspect, with all the evidence mounting against him, confessed.

Although this case was never brought to trial and Ubelaker's findings were never presented, his investigative work revealed what really happened and brought the case to a conclusion. Many of the experiments that forensic anthropologists conduct pertain to a specific criminal case, but when published they add to the overall body of knowledge about a specific weapon, or type of crime, and can be used as reference by other anthropologists.

Gunshot Trauma

Violent skeletal trauma falls into three basic categories: gunshot wounds, blunt-force trauma, and sharp-force trauma. Each type of attack leaves its signature on bone. The extent of the damage sustained by a gunshot is determined by the type of firearm and bullet, the range from which the shot was fired, its trajectory, and velocity. But in general, a skull subjected to a gunshot sustains a circular entrance hole with edges that are beveled internally. The bone shatters, causing fractures to flare out from the center of impact in a starburst pattern. If the bone fragments do not show a clear entrance or exit wound, this pattern can help establish the direction of the bullet. High-velocity weapons will produce greater fracturing than lower-velocity weapons because the gases expand more rapidly inside the cranial vault. As the bullet leaves the cranium, its contained force blasts out leaving a larger, more ragged

This skull shows the circular entrance wound of a bullet. [© Chip Clark/NMNH, Smithsonian Institution]

hole. The edges are beveled externally. The placement of the entrance and exit holes reveals the trajectory of the shot and may indicate whether the wound was self-inflicted or had to have been caused by someone else. Was the victim facing the killer or running away? Was the shot from far away or at close range? Even after being cleaned and preserved for use in a reference collection, one skull of a suicide victim still retained the distinctive dark discoloring of unburned powder around the entrance hole characteristic of a contact wound.

A shotgun blast produces a different type of wound depending on the size of the shot and the distance between muzzle and target. At close range there may be two entrance wounds that have scalloped margins and small starburst fractures. Shotgun pellets rarely leave the body and are visible on an X ray.

A gunshot to other parts of the body does not leave the same pattern of fracture, and unless the bullet is lodged in the bone, the only evidence may be shattering of long bones or nicks and depressions from metal fragments.

Blunt-Force Trauma

When a person receives a severe blow to the head with a mallet or frying pan, their skull suffers a depressed fracture that looks like a saucer-shaped crater. Bone fragments are pushed inward because the outer layer of bone is more completely fractured than the inner layer of bone. The thin cranial vault cracks in a series of concentric circles, expanding outward like rings on a shooting target. Additional fracture lines may radiate out from the epicenter surrounding the site of the initial impact, and secondary damage on the opposite side might be visible. At the moment of impact, the bone is pushed in at the site of contact and bulges out on the opposing side. A forensic anthropologist can decipher the sequence of multiple blows by examining the spiderweb of damage and mapping out the fractures that cross and interlace.

Groups of weapons share similar characteristics such as the width of a claw, the diameter of the pounding head, similar curving lines, or angles, which cause similar trauma markings. These weapons are said to have the same class characteristics. For example, there is a whole range of tire irons that can leave an imprint in the skull that is so distinctive that afterward a similar tool can be fitted into the traumatized area. When a tool has an imperfection, such as chipped paint, a roughened edge, or a missing part that can leave a unique mark on the bone,

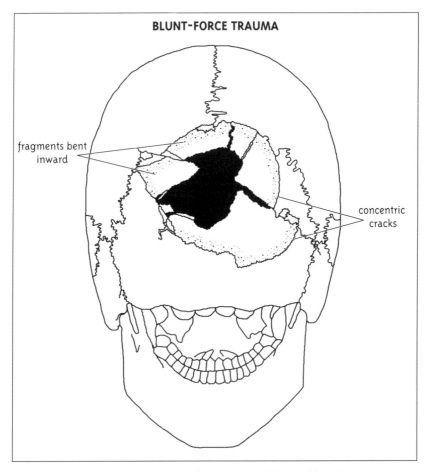

BLUNT-FORCE TRAUMA

fragments bent inward

concentric cracks

A blunt object like a block of wood or a frying pan would cause blunt-force trauma. Note the concentric cracks around the wound and the fragments that are bent inward.

it is regarded as an individual characteristic and can link a specific weapon to a wound.

Sharp-Force Trauma

When a knife is plunged into a body, it is almost certain that it will hit some bone on the way in. The ribs are a good place to look for fatal blows that have reached the heart and lungs. Wounds found on the bones of the palm and forearms indicate that the victim may have defended his or herself by holding up the arms to protect the face and body. The angle of those slashes may also suggest if the killer was right- or left-handed. And the sequence of stab wounds can be determined by examining their depth and position.

A knife can be wielded in a stabbing, slashing, or hacking motion, and each attack will yield a slightly different type of wound. A deep stab wound to the chest might leave small puncturing nicks on ribs and

Cleaning Bones

Most of the time, trauma is hidden under decomposing tissue. To see surface details and signs of injury, the flesh needs to be cleaned away, because even a thin layer of dirt and grime can obscure signs of violence. Skeletons that are recovered from long-term burials can be scrubbed gently under running water with a soft brush like a toothbrush. Working over a screen prevents loose fragments from going down the drain. For more recent cadavers that are still covered with flesh or adipocere, the bones may need to be soaked in large vats of water. Although this is time-consuming, taking several weeks, it is a noninvasive process. Every few days the murky liquid is drained off and replaced with clean water. This process is used when preparing bones with fine detail such as the pubic symphysis for research.

Because forensic anthropologists are usually under some kind of time constraint, the process is hurried along with heat. The bones are placed in vats and simmered. Some anthropologists add a gentle detergent or more caustic solution depending on the condition of the bones and how soon the work needs to be done. In a university or medical examiner's lab the skeletal preparation is carried out under large fume hoods that vent the noxious odors from the room and out of the building.

Once the flesh is removed, nothing is holding broken bones together. Shattered skulls and fractured femurs are reconstructed with glue and great patience. Duco cement, a type of model airplane glue, is frequently used because it does not expand when wet or alter the bone, but it does dissolve with acetone if a mistake is made and needs to be corrected. Reconstructing fractured bone is like assembling a fragile 3-D puzzle. Forensic anthropologists must gauge the thickness of bone walls, measure the curvature of fragments and the circumference of bone, and study the shape of the joints, protuberances, and muscle attachments in order to put all the pieces together.

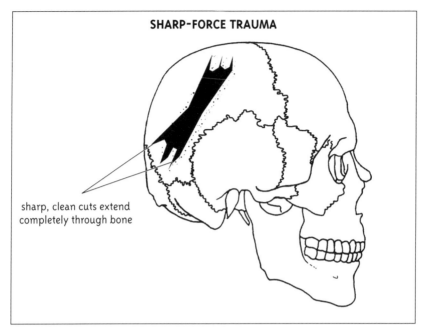

SHARP-FORCE TRAUMA

sharp, clean cuts extend
completely through bone

A knife, machete, or any object with a cutting edge will slice through bone, leaving clean margins.

even the vertebrae if the stabbing force is strong enough. A slashing motion with a sharp knife may produce fine clean cuts, while hacking splinters bone.

As the knife pushes its way through bone, it moves the hard material along with it, leaving the back edge of the cut splintery, just as a saw through wood leaves the back edge rough and jagged. This can be felt with the fingertips and indicates the direction of the attack. As the blade is removed, the wound closes, leaving a cut mark that is narrower than the blade.

A microscopic view of a cut can reveal even more about the type of knife and how it was used. Depending on what they were made for, different classes of knives produce different markings—thin lines, or striations—on the wall of a cut called the kerf wall. Serrated knives produce a narrow scalloped-edged groove with fine, smooth striations on the kerf wall. Courser and larger knives create more noticeable striations. In cross section, a sharp knife makes a V-shaped cut, and a dull knife creates a U-shaped dent.

According to the *Sourcebook of Criminal Statistics*, in 1999, 13.2 percent of all murders and nonnegligent manslaughter cases known to the police in the United States were carried out with a knife or other cutting tool. But most research reports describing skeletal trauma have come from 14th and 17th century historic cases uncovered at archaeological sites. To document hacking trauma as it pertains to modern crime, Joshua Humphrey and Dale Hutchinson conducted an experiment to record the subtle differences between cleaver, machete, and ax wounds when applied to the limbs of a fully fleshed dead pig.

After several strikes with each instrument, the pig's limbs were cleaned to reveal the skeletal trauma underneath. Cleaver wounds only partially penetrated the bone and left recognizable entry sites that were narrow, clean, and smooth. The machete produced much chattering or bone chipping and a medium-sized entry site. An ax blow crushed the bone and caused extensive fracturing. Microscopic analysis showed fine, thin striations along the edges of a cleaver wound and course, rugged marks on the machete wound. The ax, which shattered the bone completely, left no visible striations.

The trauma from another class of weapon, the saw, is just as varied as the many tools on the market. There are meat saws, surgical stryker saws, wood saws, hacksaws, handsaws, power saws, circular saws, and many more. And, unfortunately, they have all, at one time or another, been used to dismember a body. In general, a saw blade creates a square-shaped cut wider than the blade itself because it chews out a path

A cut mark made by a knife. [Kathleen O. Arries]

through bone. In cross section, a wound created by a circular saw will have fine curved lines, a wound left from a saber saw will leave regular straight cuts, and handsaws characteristically make straight but uneven striations.

Evidence of Child Abuse

Until recently, very little attention has been given to identifying chronic abuse in the skeletal remains of children, even though these types of cases are common. It is not unusual for an abusive parent who has killed a child to hide the body or keep the remains for many years.

Five years after first being reported missing, the partially skeletonized remains of a three-year-old boy were discovered in the trunk of his parents' car. Initially, the parents told police that their child had died accidentally while taking a bath and they buried him. But it soon became evident that they had carried his body in their car the whole time. When the initial autopsy, conducted by the pathologist, was inconclusive as to how the boy died, the parents were only charged with illegally disposing of human remains. A forensic anthropologist was then asked to examine the bones. While pathologists and radiographers are able to document perimortem trauma, recent reports suggest that chronic abuse results in lesions that are not visible on X rays but are visible when decomposed tissue is removed and the bones are examined by an anthropologist. In this case, the forensic anthropologist was able to document several signs of prior trauma suggesting chronic child abuse.

On the three-year-old's skull was a linear fracture that showed at least several weeks of healing. Superimposed on this was a second partially healed fracture that occurred only a week or so prior to death. The right clavicle had a fully healed fracture suggesting that it had occurred long before either skull fracture, and the left radius and ulna showed signs of lesions and new bone growth indicating that at one time this area had been badly bruised or abraded. X rays of the long bones showed Harris lines, fine markings indicating that the child's growth was interrupted then started again. This is commonly found in children who have been chronically abused, suffered a prolonged illness, psychological stress, or poor nutrition. His teeth, too, showed fine lines called lines of Retzius, supporting the theory of interrupted growth. Because of these findings, the parents were charged with their son's murder and eventually pleaded guilty.

Evidence of chronic child abuse in skeletal remains is character-ized by a combination of multiple fractures on different parts of the body, especially in various stages of healing, bone lesions, Harris lines on bone, and lines of Retzius on teeth. Abused children under three commonly show bruising of head and neck bones, as well as rib frac-tures absent of major chest trauma. This type of injury results from grasping a small child around the chest and shaking or squeezing. Shaking also causes chip fractures of the joints of the knee and elbows, and forcefully grabbing and twisting a limb causes spiral frac-tures. Now that skeletal trauma has been more fully documented, perhaps more cases of child abuse and murder will come to trial.

Burned Bone

Many of the cases that forensic anthropologists work on involve burned bone, because fire consumes the flesh leaving little for a pathol-ogist to work with. It contorts the remains and eventually renders them fragile fragments. Even so, they still hold a wealth of information.

Many people believe that fire can burn a body completely, but what they don't know is that a fire would need to be well above 2,500 degrees F for more than 18 hours in order to get the job done. A typ-ical house fire burns at 900 to 1,800 degrees F and usually lasts no more than six to eight hours.

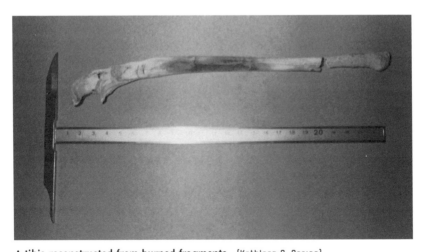

A tibia reconstructed from burned fragments. [Kathleen O. Arries]

When a body is exposed to fire, the heat contracts the muscles, forcing them to flex. The legs pull into a crouch, and the arms come up in a fighting stance. This is called the pugilistic position. Longer exposure to high temperatures burns the flesh away and causes the moisture in the bone to expand. The long bones will crack and warp, and the pressure inside the skull builds up until it explodes, sending fragments a great distance. Each bone reacts differently because of its size and density. Some bones such as the tibia fracture into cubes like a checkerboard pattern. The femur with its thicker outer layer of bone cracks into little crescent shapes. The long bones shrink in size up to one-quarter their original length, and thin bones such as the ribs can be reduced to stubs.

Burned bones also change color. As the organic compounds are burned away, the bones turn from creamy white to dark yellow, to black, to gray, and finally to white. When they are white, they are said to be calcined, only calcium carbonate and other minerals are left. In 1985, when William Maples was faced with more than 10,000 burned bone fragments, he used the fragment's color, shape, size, and texture to piece together the commingled remains. It took more than a year to reconstruct the remains of the male and female who died in the fire.

It is unusual for a fire to be so intense and so prolonged as to completely destroy a body. Even in a crematorium the fire may not obliterate all identifying characteristics. That is done by a processor, or pulverizing machine, once the bones are cooled. Forensic anthropologists are occasionally asked to consult on cases where a family is not certain it received the correct remains, or *cremains*, from a crematorium. In these instances, the ashes are sifted and great pains are taken to find any bone fragment large enough to elicit any type of identifying feature, such as arthritic growths, tooth fragments, a dental post used to hold a crown in place, or the presence of surgical staples. There have even been studies done on the differences in weight of the ashes of a male versus a female body. Even at this stage of fragmentation, some evidence of a person's identity may still be visible.

After the Fire

In 1993, a religious cult called the Branch Davidians holed up inside the walls of its Texas compound after federal law officers demanded the surrender of the group's firearms. The leader of the group, David Koresh, held the marshals at bay for nearly two months, before federal troops broke down the compound's walls with tanks and threw tear gas in hopes that Koresh and his followers would run out. But that did not happen, instead, the buildings burst into flames and burned to the ground. When the fires subsided, 86 people had died. Rumors spread that the religious leaders had killed some of their followers, and there had been a mass suicide. Other rumors said that the federal government had murdered the people by starting the fire. What really happened? Was Koresh dead, or had he escaped through underground tunnels as it was rumored? Only the bones would tell.

Along with FBI agents, Texas rangers and staff from the Tarrant County Medical Examiner's office, Smithsonian anthropologists Douglas Ubelaker and Douglas Owsley excavated the smoldering rubble and sifted the ashes. They placed little red flags to mark where each body was found. The remains were badly charred and many were beyond recognition, so the forensic team went to work sorting through hundreds of bones establishing age and sex. Postmortem X rays were matched with antemortem medical records. Eventually, two sets of remains found lying near each other in what was once the communication room were identified as those of David Koresh and his right-hand man, David Schneider. Toxicology reports confirmed that they were still alive when the fire started, but both suffered a gunshot wound to the head. Koresh's skull showed an entrance wound about 1 inch above the brow ridge and an exit wound out the back of the head. Schneider had a clear exit wound at the back of the head, but no clear entrance wound. The medical examiner speculated that the entrance may have been in the mouth. The trajectory of the exit and entrance holes suggested that the bullets were fired at close range but could not conclusively determine suicide or homicide.

Many of the bodies of Koresh's followers, who were recovered from the house and bunker, showed that they died of smoke inhalation and blunt-force trauma when debris collapsed in on them. But in all, 20 people, including three children, died from gunshot wounds, and one toddler was fatally stabbed. More than eight years later, gossip and rumors still circulate about what happened, but in the end the bones—even charred ones—speak for themselves.

The Case of the Body in the Burned-Out Car

On Christmas Day, 1988, deer hunters found the remains of a burned-out car, but it wasn't until the next day after a second closer look that they saw burned bone fragments, teeth, and a Seiko watch where the front seat once was. The sheriff's department called in Dr. Edward Waldrip, the director of the Southern Institute of Forensic Science, to look at the remains. From the damage to the bones and the car, Waldrip estimated that the fire had burned as hot as 2,000 degrees F for at least two hours.

The few fragments sifted from the charred rubble told Waldrip that the victim had been a man with a small build. There was so little left of the man that Waldrip was forced to use an arm bone to calculate height. An arm bone is not a very accurate indicator of height, but it told Waldrip that the man was between 5 feet 4 inches to 5 feet 10 inches tall. The man was 25 to 30 years old, give or take five years. He

Edward Waldrip sits at a table full of burned bone fragments. He pieces them back together like a skeletal jigsaw puzzle.
(Kathleen O. Arries)

was also disabled. "He had a markedly smaller left leg," Waldrip said. "The bones of the knee were also smaller on the left." The man would have walked with a limp.

There were no other signs of trauma on the skull, rib, or chest fragments to indicate anything other than suicide, but there was so little left of the body that homicide could not be ruled out just yet.

While Waldrip examined the bones, the sheriff's department tried to find the owner of the burned-out car. They knew it was a Fiat, but all other identifying numbers and license plates had been removed. The Fiat company in Italy informed the police of a secret registration number that the owner may not have been aware of. The number was still on the car and led the police to a Fiat dealership in California and then to the original owner who claimed she had sold the car to a Vietnamese man.

Once the sheriff had the name of the owner, the rest of the pieces fell into place. Relatives described the man as small, about 5 feet 6 inches tall and weighing only 100 pounds. He was 32 years old and suffered from muscular dystrophy, a disease that causes the muscles to gradually deteriorate. In fact, the last time he was seen, at Thanksgiving, the man had mentioned being so disabled that he was contemplating suicide. Members of his family remembered he also wore a Seiko watch.

A check on the man uncovered that he had been arrested in 1986 near Billings, Montana, for having no identification on the car and for having 50 pipe bombs, gasoline, charcoal briquettes, and gunpowder in the car. He told police that he intended to commit suicide and leave no evidence behind because he did not want to live with the advanced stages of muscular dystrophy. It seems that two years later he was still intent on his plan, but this time no one was there to stop him.

FACE FINDING

The dead skull is, in a sense, the matrix of the living head.

—Wilton M. Krogman and M. Y. İşcan,
The Human Skeleton in Forensic Medicine, 1986

There is a saying that beauty is skin deep. That may be true, but the design of the face goes to the bone. Whether you have a jutting chin, high cheeks, a narrow nose, large eyes, or a big smile is all determined by the contours of the skull.

The first scientists to pursue this were 19th-century German anatomists like Wilhelm His, who in 1895 studied the heads of 24 male and four female cadavers. It seems gruesome, but his research required him to stick pins into various points on the face until he struck the bone. Marking the pin and pulling it out again, he could measure the thickness of the tissue, skin, fat, and muscle that make up the face.

Dr. His discovered that the thickness of the tissue varied on different parts of the face; the skin that cushions the cheek, for example, is thicker than that stretching over the forehead but thinner than the tissue padding the chin. You can find that out by feeling your own face, but Dr. His's real discovery was that the thickness of flesh on each part of the face remained fairly constant from person to person. For instance, the faces of Caucasian men measured up like this: The depth of tissue at the thickest spot, which is just below the nose and above the upper lip, was 11½ millimeters. The thinnest spot, which is one-third of the way down the nose where the nasal bone ends and the cartilage begins, was only 2 millimeters deep. If all of our skin measures up the same, then why do we all look so different? Dr. His decided that the determining factor was not the flesh but the bone underneath.

Dr. His believed he could apply clay to an actual skull and construct a recognizable face. The skull he wished to reconstruct was thought to be that of Johann Sebastian Bach, the great 18th-century composer who had been dead and decomposing for more than 100 years by the time Dr. His finished the facial reconstruction. Dr. His relied on a sculptor to translate the skull tissue measurements onto the actual skull, and the end result was a bust that looked surprisingly similar to Bach. It became popular to reconstruct historic faces, and by the turn of the century, the faces of Kant, Raphael, and Dante had all been sculpted in this manner. Russian scientists called it "face finding," because it is always a surprise to the artists when they finally see the face that they have been working on.

Facial reconstruction, or *facial approximation* as it is referred to now, was not used for forensic purposes in the United States until the 1940s. Forensic anthropologists thought that if reconstructing a famous person's face attracted such public attention, then perhaps the approximation of an unknown person could spark a memory; a wife might recognize her husband, or a father might recognize his child. It's a last ditch effort in identifying a corpse with no identifying features, no name, and no one coming forward to claim it.

Finding Frank

In 1981, in Chautauqua County in western New York State, a body was found wrapped up in a sleeping bag. The body was that of a man wearing a denim jacket and jeans with a western-style leather belt hand tooled with the inscription "Frank." There was no other identification. It was not a pretty sight. Decomposition of the body had been delayed by the sleeping bag, and inside it, the remains had liquefied into a putrid brown goo. The face, which had been exposed to the elements, was gone, but it was apparent that Frank had been shot twice in the head. Who was this man?

The county medical examiner viewed the remains, but with no clue as to who they represented, the man would be buried as a John Doe.

Kathleen Arries, a forensic anthropologist who consulted with the medical examiner and sheriff's department, pulled the remains from the morgue freezer to see how she could help.

The skull was distinctive. On the left side of the mandible, between the chin and jaw, there was a deformation that looked as if a great gouge had been taken out, but the bone had just grown that way. Arries decided that the skull would make a prime candidate for a reconstruction, because some of the most successful reconstructions are made with skulls that have a distinguishing feature, such as a jutting jaw, a healed trauma that would indicate a noticeable scar during life, or a gold tooth.

Arries noticed markings on the other facial bones that the medical examiner had dismissed as postmortem rodent chew marks. A closer look convinced her that the marks were made with a knife because they were all parallel, evenly spaced, equally deep, and made at right angles. After killing this man, someone had taken the time to scrape the skin off his face so that he would never be identified. To Arries, the case was a challenge that she could not pass up. Reconstructing the dead man's skull would offer him one last chance of being recognized.

Unlike many facial reconstructionists, Arries preferred to work on a plaster cast of the skull rather than the skull itself. That way the skull is not damaged, and it allows more than one person to work on the skull at the same time. A latex and gauze casting was made and then split off to use as a mold to make a plaster skull. With the chart listing the reference points and tissue depths to adult Caucasian males next to her, Arries began to work.

Researchers have developed standardized tissue depths for 21 points of the skull. For each reference point, Arries cut a small piece of plasticine to the proper length. The markers, which resemble the eraser at the end of a pencil, are placed on the skull, making it look like an odd form of skeletal acupuncture.

Strips of clay are then placed on the skull connecting the 21 points. Positioning this lattice work is like playing connect the dots in three dimensions. The important part is to keep the clay strips the appropriate thickness. As the surrounding areas are filled in and smoothed out, the face begins to take shape.

Arries selected eyes from a small carrying case filled with different size glass eyeballs—blue, green, hazel, and brown, each in its own velvet pocket. Arries chose the most common eye color, brown. Contrary to what most people think, eyeballs are pretty much the same size.

FACE POINTS

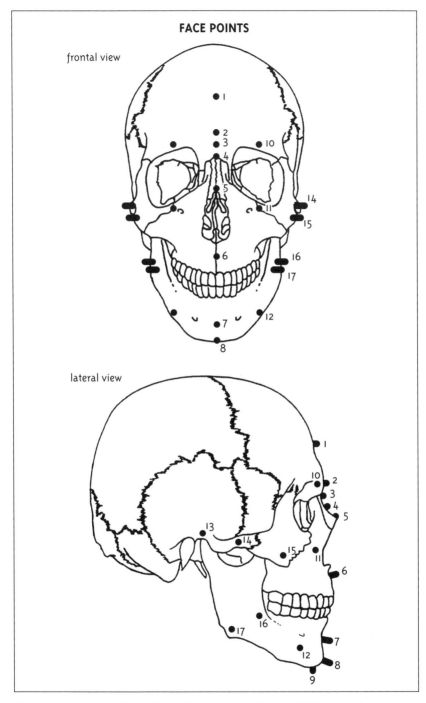

There are 21 points on the skull that have calculated tissue thicknesses. These points are used as reference when approximating a face from a skull.

They grow only slightly from infancy to adulthood. The illusion of big eyes or little eyes is mostly due to the size of the eye opening in the bone, called the orbit.

From this point on, Arries had to rely on her art training. Although the bone dictates the contours of the face, it is difficult to determine the shape and size of the nose, the fullness of the lips, and the design of the ears. The underlying bone gives only subtle suggestions about these features, general guidelines that the sculptor follows. The size and shape of the nose, for example, is suggested by the size and shape of the nasal opening. Research suggests that the shape of the nose can be predicted with approximately 60 percent accuracy, and the shape of the tip of the nose at only 40 percent accuracy. And there are two schools of thought on how that nose as well as other features are approximated, the Gerasimov method developed by the Russian paleontologist Mikhail Gerasimov and the American method practiced by most artists and anthropologists in the United States. Those who practice the Gerasimov method take their cue from the basic shape of the nasal opening. The cartilage that supports the tent-like stretch of skin on the nose decays along with the tissue, leaving a large triangular-shaped gap. The edge of the opening curves gently outward suggesting where the nose once projected forward. Those who practice the Gerasimov method extend one line from the bridge of the nose and a second line from the small arrow-shaped bit of bone called the spine that juts out at the base of the nose, and then round their point of intersection to make the tip.

The American school relies more on statistics. The spine of the nose acts as a support and is approximately one-third of the actual length of the nose. In a Caucasian male, the nose is about one-third wider than the nasal opening. Knowing this, Arries could estimate the width and length. Betty Pat Gatliff, a forensic artist who has been creating facial approximations for more than 35 years, relies on mathematical formulae to derive facial measurements. The width of the fleshed nose, for example, is found by measuring across the nasal aperture and increasing that measurement by 10 millimeters, 5 on either side. The projection of the nose is calculated by measuring the tiny projection of bone at the base of the nose just above the lip and multiplying it by three.

The mouth is roughly as wide as the distance between the pupils of the eyes, but the lips are unpredictable. Arries constructed a generic-looking mouth with the lips closed. The ear is also made of cartilage that decomposes quickly, but estimates on living people show that the ear, from the top to the lobe, is approximately as long as a person's nose. Did the man have dangling earlobes or were they attached? Did his ears stick out or hug the head closely? Again Arries sculpted generic-looking ears.

A forensic artist would be negligent not to incorporate racial attributes into an approximation. For this Caucasian male, Arries sculpted a narrow, long nose and thin lips, but on a Negroid skull she may have made the lips a little fuller, and she would have given an Asian male the slight folds over the eyes characteristic of Asians. Facial approximations may seem to follow stereotypes, but these characteristics have to be considered to get the best result, namely that someone will recognize the unknown person. If the skull belonged to an elderly person, wrinkles and a slight sag of the skin on the neck would have been added for a more authentic appearance. Was the person heavy or thin? Often times clothes, a belt, ring, or hat may give some indication of the person's size, but forensic facial reconstructionist Karen Taylor notes that this is not always true because of the recent teen trend of wearing oversized clothes. In the absence of tangible evidence of size, the artist simply creates a face of average weight.

To create skin texture, fine-grain sandpaper is gently blotted on the smooth clay. The last step is the hair. Wigs never look completely natural, but they are necessary to the approximation process. Arries combed out a man's brown wig that matched the color of a strand of hair found on the skeleton. She photographed the bust for the police to distribute and then added the sunglasses that were found in the dead man's shirt pocket and photographed it again. No one knows what factor will be crucial in determining the identity of a face—it could be as simple as sunglasses.

The police added the photos to the homicide file, but no one came forward to identify him. Eleven years later, an informant in Ohio told police about a 10-year-old murder and how the victim had been dumped in a field. The circumstances were similar to those surrounding the Chautauqua homicide, and the murdered man's name was Frank. Arries's sculpture helped to corroborate Frank's identity, but it could not stand alone in court. A state trooper close to the case noted years later that " . . . the reconstruction and drawing were remarkably similar to the man's photograph." Finally, on Thursday, October 1, 1992, the district attorney of Chautauqua County issued a statement identifying Frank as a 46-year-old man from Painsville, Ohio, whose body had been dumped in New York. The killer was arrested and convicted, and Frank's remains were returned to his family.

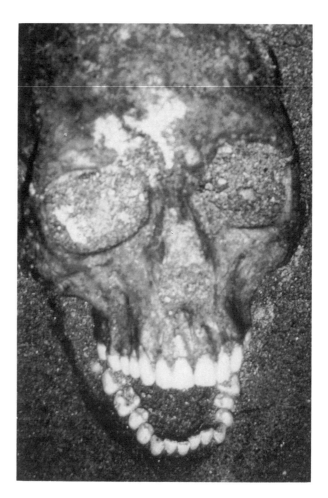

The skull of a War of 1812 soldier excavated from his grave. The slackened jaw earned him the nickname **Grinner.** (Kathleen O. Arries)

Grinner—a Face from the Past

The same forensic techniques are often used to bring to life a face from the past. In 1987, an unmarked cemetery was uncovered during the construction of a new house on the shores of Lake Erie in Canada. It turned out that the site had once been a burial ground for dead soldiers during the War of 1812. An archaeological team was assigned the job of recovering the bodies and identifying them as best they could. Twenty-eight skeletons were exhumed, and from the insignias on the buttons found among the bones, it appeared that they were American soldiers. Each skeleton showed signs of battle injuries or medical treatment, such as musket fire, cannon blasts, and amputation.

The second soldier to be uncovered had a full set of teeth that gleamed white against the dark brown soil, and as it is with all skeletons, after the ligaments of the jaw decayed, his heavy mandible

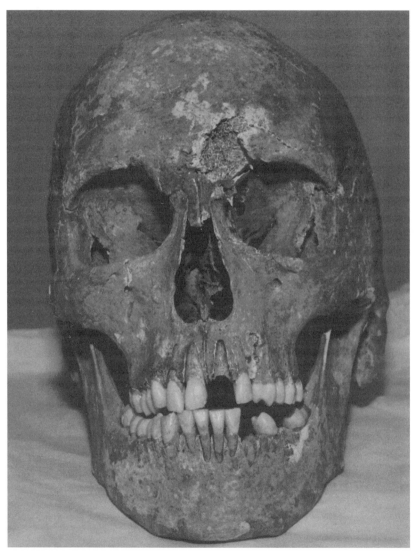

Grinner's skull is cleaned and ready for the anthropologist to make a facial approximation. [Kathleen O. Arries]

The skull is covered in latex and gauze to make a mold. (Kathleen O. Arries)

dropped to the chest, giving him a gaping grin. The archaeological team nicknamed him Grinner.

Grinner had been buried with his feet bound and hands folded across his stomach. Under his right shoulder blade was a copper pin that may have held closed a bandage, suggesting that Grinner had been in a military hospital before he died.

Of all of the skeletons, Grinner's skull was in the best shape; some of the other skulls had been destroyed by cannon fire or were missing altogether. Grinner was a good candidate for an approximation. The anthropologist chose to give Grinner blue eyes and reddish brown hair because U.S. Army records indicated that these were the most common features among the soldiers at the time. Now visitors to Fort Erie, Canada, can actually see the face of one of the soldiers who slept in the barracks, stood guard in the towers, fought, and died in the War of 1812.

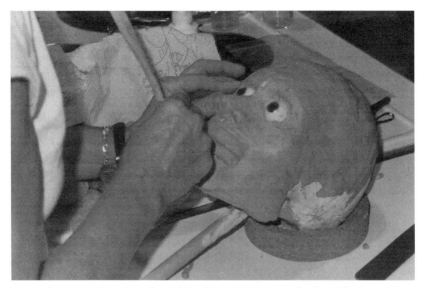

Strips of clay are placed on the mold and smoothed out to the desired tissue depths. [Kathleen O. Arries]

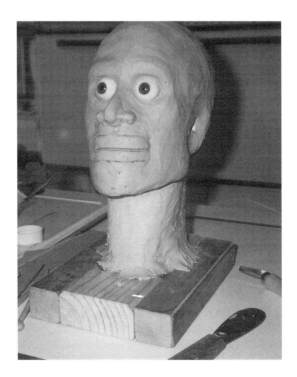

Applying the nose, lips, and ears takes an artist's touch. [Kathleen O. Arries]

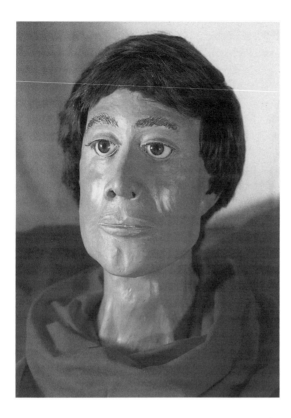

The finished approxima-
tion of Grinner as he
might have looked
before his death in 1812.
(Kathleen O. Arries)

New Standards

For more than one hundred years, some scientists have questioned the usefulness and the validity of applying clay to a skull to derive an accurate portrait of a person. The term facial reconstruction has been changed to facial approximation because the procedure admittedly cannot reliably re-create a person's face. One of the primary concerns regarding the method's accuracy is the fact that the tissue depth data that forensic anthropologists and artists rely on are based on cadavers. Decomposition studies have recorded significant and rapid changes in the human body after death, especially loss of fluids from the face. Tissue depths taken from cadavers would therefore be inaccurate and would yield faces that were less fleshy than the person in life.

Much of the original data also came primarily from a small population of older Caucasian males. Studies that included both sexes, people of other races, or different ages did not appear until recently. For many years, these limited measurement standards were applied erroneously to faces of every nationality, sex, and age.

The standard measurements were revised over the decades, but all studies to determine tissue depth still used cadavers and the needle technique. In the 1980s, scientists took advantage of new methods of data collection such as CAT scans, magnetic resonance imaging (MRI), ultrasound, and images of craniographs taken of the living. Recently Mary Manheim, director of the Louisiana State University's Forensic Anthropology and Computer Enhancement Services (FACES) Lab, led a two-year study of living people to update facial tissue depth measurements for American adults and children. They measured the faces of more than 250 adults and 500 children who visited the pediatric clinic at the Louisiana State University Medical Center, School of Dentistry in New Orleans. The participant's face was scanned at 19 points using ultrasound technology similar to that used in obstetrics. Calipers within the ultrasound machine measured the distance between the surface of the skin to the bone underneath in centimeters and millimeters. The research showed that for some points that were measured, there was a significant difference in tissue depths between sexes, races, and age. There was a significant relationship between age and tissue depths at 16 of 19 points for Caucasians, 17 of 19 for African Americans, and 8 of 19 points for Hispanics. The point between the eyes, for example, is related to gender—white males vary from all other groups, while black females differed from only white and black males. The point next to the nostril is influenced by age in white adults, but not in African-American adults. The greatest deviation exists in the cheek region and might account for less-than-accurate facial approximations.

Computer Imaging

Long before three-dimensional approximations were made, police relied on sketch artists to render two-dimensional drawings of a suspect or to "clean up" the image of murder victims at the morgue. Face kits, such as Identi-Kit, were developed consisting of predrawn facial features that a witness could select from. These methods relied on an eyewitness, but forensic anthropologists and artists also developed ways to approximate a two-dimensional face from just the skull, using the same data that is used for 3-D sculptures. The most common method involved tracing the image of the skull from a radiograph or a photograph, plotting the correct tissue depth markers, drawing the subsequent face, and adding detail. Two-dimensional drawings were less time consuming than sculpting and were easy to circulate.

Computer-assisted facial approximations, however, are growing more common, and there are a number of software packages on the market that work in the same way. A forensic anthropologist places tissue depth markers on the skull and scans the image into the computer to form a template. Then clay is applied and the general features are sculpted. The computer is used primarily to enhance the features, make quick alterations, and to create multiple variations of the image that show the individual with slightly different-shaped ears, nose, or lips or views from different angles. Different hair color and styles can be applied, and any jewelry, clothing, or eyeglasses that may have been associated with the body can be included.

Software such as CARES (Computer Assisted Reconstruction and Enhancement System), Faces, and FACE store an image from a radiograph of a skull or photograph and build the face using selected facial features from a databank. Other programs scan a skull as it rotates on a platform. The image is converted to a matrix of latitude and longitude that creates a wire-frame skull. Tissue depth measurements are then used to generate the facial approximation. Digitized images of facial features are added as are color and texture.

Critics of computer-generated images question the accuracy of facial features because the computer can only select from a series of images, and the underlying bones do not adequately generate the information for those features. Martin Evison, from the University of Sheffield, England, warns:

> Although the results are more reproducible than sculpted reconstructions, some subjectivity can remain in the "pegging" of a composite facial image onto the digitized skull matrix. The use of such a standardized image will reduce the influence of the individual shape of each skull, which is after all fundamental to the person's appearance. Computerized methods may be repeatable, fast and precise, but as long as they employ the old data, the quality of the reconstruction will be undermined.

However, computers are an asset when fragmented skulls need to be reconstructed, because the fragments can be scanned and manipulated without further damaging the remains.

What Are the Chances?

Facial approximations have always sat on the edge between science and art, but recent studies have tried to quantify their reliability. One study conducted in Australia suggested that faces built from dry skulls were not recognized above chance rates. Sixteen faces were created from four skulls using four different commonly used methods, including two 3-D sculpture methods, 2-D manual drawing, and 2-D computerized image. Each of the approximations were viewed by 37 people who were then asked to choose the matching subject from 10 accompanying photos. Only one approximation elicited a true positive identification above chance rates. This study was of a small sample size and simply offered forensic scientists something to think about, but it does run contrary to the track record claimed by sculptors and artists who create facial approximations. Anthropologist Clyde Snow and artist Betty Pat Gatliff have created many approximations and reported that 19 out of 22 cases were successfully identified. Other anthropologists report success rates of 25 percent to 50 percent and suggest that successful conclusions may be due to the inclusion of additional information such as hair, jewelry, or clothing that sparked the recognition. But no matter what the odds are, when there are no other avenues of identifying an unidentified body any chance is better than none.

Photographic Superimposition

Facial reconstructions are made when the police have no clue as to the identity of a skeleton, but sometimes the police do have an idea who the person may turn out to be, because of unsolved missing person cases or from an airplane's passenger list. In such instances, they are able to corroborate identity using a photographic technique called *superimposition*. This method compares a photograph of the suspected missing person with a skull thought to belong to the individual.

One of the earliest cases that involved photographic superimposition was a gruesome murder that took place in England in the mid-1930s. Two skulls, two torsos, 17 parts of limbs, and 43 slabs of soft tissue were collected from a riverbank near Moffat, Scotland, and later identified as two females. The suspected identities were Isabella Van Ess and her maid, Mary Rogerson, reported missing just days

Video equipment for superimposition. The monitor in the center blends the photographic image on the left with the image of the skull on the right. [© William R. Maples, courtesy of Margaret Maples Gilliland]

before. The prime suspect was Miss Van Ess's common-law-husband, Dr. Buck Ruxton.

The bodies had not only been dismembered, but the murderer took great care to remove all identifying marks. Fingertips were cut off from one set of hands to prevent fingerprinting, and the eyes were removed from a skull, presumably to prevent the discovery of the maid's noticeable squint. Even a bunion had been removed from one of the feet. It seemed that the murderer had obliterated every means of identification—except one. A photograph of the two women had been found in the Buxton home, and Dr. John Glaister and Dr. James Couper Brash reconstructed the bodies and posed them in the same positions and photographed them. The images of the women's faces were then superimposed onto the photograph of the mutilated skulls to reveal clearly that the images were from the same two women. Ruxton was subsequently arrested and convicted of the double murder.

Today, superimposition is accomplished by using two video cameras connected to a mixer or by scanning two images into a computer with specially designed software. The images can then be moved on and off screen, made clearer, or faded out. The mixer can produce the effect of a split screen, with a line that runs horizontally or vertically between both images at the same time, or half of each image. The line can be moved to show more of one image and less of another across the screen. This is called a "wipe." A "fade" is like a dream sequence in a movie, as one image blurs and fades to expose the other image. The fade can be equalized so that both the portrait and the skull can be seen as if the person's skin were transparent.

There are many points on the skull that can be compared with the photo to prove that they are of the same person, but each spot must match up exactly. Starting at the bottom of the skull, the center of the jawbone must match up with the point of the chin. The bite line of the teeth on the skull should be even with the lip line on the photograph. The nasal opening should be the same shape and length as the actual nose. Working upward, the position of the eyeballs is checked. They should be centered in the orbits. At the outside of the eye, on the outer margin, there is a muscle attachment that you can feel by running your finger up the side of your eye socket. Feel at the top where the bone abruptly turns toward the back of the head. On some people, this line is visible and can be matched with the bone structure on the skull. The small opening of the ear canal on the skull should align with the ear canal as observed in the photograph. If even one point on the skull is misaligned, the police have to resume their search.

The accuracy of superimposition has not been studied extensively, but one experiment conducted at the C. A. Pound Human ID Laboratory of the Florida Museum of Natural History at the University of Florida looked at the reliability of superimposition to determine a perfect match. One hundred mug shots of criminals were superimposed onto three totally unrelated skulls. In eight cases a match of the skull with a photograph occurred in one view. The front views matched

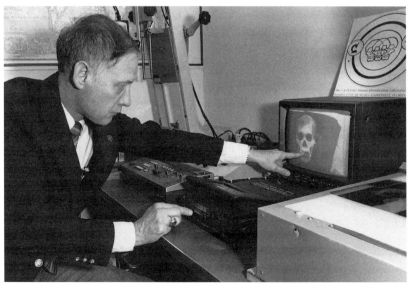

William Maples points out areas of comparison on a superimposed image.
[University of Florida News & Public Affairs]

while the side view did not, or the side view matched and the front view did not. In only one instance was a match made in both views. In 99 percent of the cases a match on more than one photograph would mean a positive identification. This study not only demonstrated the chances for error in superimpositions, but also the need for scientists to use more than one method of identification.

Aging in an adult does not affect the identification process at all. As we get older, earlobes lengthen, the tip of the nose droops, wrinkles crease the forehead and the area around the eyes, and the skin loosens and sags, but all this happens on the surface. The inner bone structure

---

Mitch Boyer

General George Armstrong Custer led the Seventh Calvary during the Battle of Little Bighorn against the Sioux and Cheyenne, and he died on what is now called Custer Hill at Custer's Last Stand on June 2, 1876. More than 267 soldiers and civilians died on the plains that day, along with many Sioux and Cheyenne. There were no survivors from the U.S. Army to tell about the events of the battle, but when troops arrived days later, the bodies they found strewn across the hills were buried where they lay.

Over 100 years, bones from those graves have been uncovered by brush fire, pushed up by heaving frost, and dug up by archaeologists. Most of the bones were fragmented and scattered. In 1985, Clyde Snow took an interest in the osteobiographies of the soldiers on the hill, and he went to the battlefield to see if any of the remains could be identified. One small fragment only 4 inches long and 2 inches wide looked promising. It was the upper jawbone with eight teeth still intact. The nasal aperture was not characteristically Caucasoid as Snow would have suspected the soldier to be. It was Mongoloid-shaped, which indicated that maybe the man was a Sioux or Cheyenne, but the teeth were not shovel shaped as Mongoloid teeth usually are. It was a puzzle. Snow checked through the historical records and came up with one man, Mitch Boyer, who was an interpreter and scout for Custer's men.

Boyer's father was French, and his mother was Santee Sioux, which would explain the mix in racial characteristics. In the historical records, there was a photograph that could be used for a superimposition. The skull fragment was small, but it offered a lot for comparison, and the pieces fit. The nasal opening lined up with the nose, the eyes sat in the middle of the eye socket, and the lips and teeth lined up perfectly.

remains the same. However, children's facial bones are changing and growing so rapidly that superimposition is less accurate in their identification. Superimposition would not work, for example, using a photo taken of a child at 10 years of age if that child died at age 15.

The best kind of photograph to use for superimposition is one in which the person is smiling. A person's teeth are unique because of all the dental irregularities and imperfections we all possess. Superimposition corroborated the identification of a North Carolina prison guard missing for four years, as well as an army scout dead for more than 125 years.

Age Progression

The Forensic Anthropology and Computer Enhancement Services (FACES) Lab at Louisiana State University not only performs skeletal analysis and facial approximations but also houses a Model Age Progression site, which is associated with the National Center for Missing or Exploited Children. Eileen Barrow, a certified age progression specialist, can take a photograph of a child and morph it into an older child or adult. All Barrow needs is the specially designed software called Photosketch and three images, one of the child at the time of his or her disappearance, and photos of both parents taken at the age their child would currently be. For example, if a three-year-old child disappeared five years ago, then the photos of the parents would need to have been taken when they were eight years old. Barrow scans in the photo of the parent the child most closely resembles and merges it slowly through a grid system from beneath the image of the child. Once the aged image is created, she can then enhance it by adding contemporary clothing, hairstyle, and other appropriate features.

The lab's director, Mary Manheim, explains that "for those children who enter our laboratory in boxes or in bags, there is no hope; for those who are missing and unaccounted for, hope drives us steadily, though warily, toward our goal—finding them alive. Few jobs evoke such strong emotion as the search for missing children. Though all such searches do not have happy endings, some do." In the first few years of performing age progressions, Dr. Manheim's lab was able to help law enforcement reunite two children with their families.

Adults have also successfully been age progressed. In 1997, the FBI requested an age progression of a man they suspected in the 1973 murder of former Louisiana state senator H. Alva Brumfield. The man eluded capture, but the case remained open until FBI agents got

The Age Progression Process

Step 1. This child disappeared at age five. Her photograph is age progressed to 20 years old using family and reference photographs. [Bureau of Missing and Exploited Children]

Step 2. A photo of the missing child's sister at age 19 is obtained. [Bureau of Missing and Exploited Children]

Step 3. The missing child's image is merged with that of the older sister. [Bureau of Missing and Exploited Children]

Step 4. A reference image of adult dentition is added. [Bureau of Missing and Exploited Children]

Step 5. A reference image of adult hair is added. [Bureau of Missing and Exploited Children]

Step 6. The final age-progressed image of the missing child at age 20. [Bureau of Missing and Exploited Children] a lead from Texas. The FBI had a Department of Motor Vehicles photograph of the man in Texas but wanted to know if it would match an age-progressed picture of the suspected killer. Eileen Barrow carefully aged the 1973 photograph and sent it to the FBI. A year later, she was informed that the photo and the age progression were enough of a match to warrant picking up their suspect. More than 20 years after his crime, Thomas Gordon Jones, alias Paul Joseph Banks of Texas, was arrested for murder.

Facial Image Identification

Another growing field in forensic anthropology is facial image identification. Surveillance cameras routinely catch criminals in the act of robbing convenience stores or holding up banks, and the images captured on film are often used to establish a person's identity through anthropometric analysis, morphological comparisons, and face-to-face superimpositions. Surveillance images are usually taken from above, so it is difficult to compare faces with a traditional mug shot that is taken at eye level. Research biologists in Japan have developed computer systems that can manipulate a mug-shot image to correspond to the same orientation of the image from a surveillance video. They measure angles of the face and compare up to 18 points to determine a match.

In the future, computers will play an increasingly larger role in facial identification and approximations. New tissue depth data and computer-based programs will allow anthropologists to create, more rapidly, an accurate digital image based on the structure of the skull or compare antemortem and postmortem images. But there is an added problem. "We do not know exactly what it is that makes a face recognizable," write Dr. Kathleen Reichs and Emily Craig. "So it remains to be seen whether computer techniques will prove more effective than current practices."

THE LAST WORD

Yet he had endured. Even his bad teeth had outlasted the outlaw state that had slain him, then tried to hide him away forever in the name-less darkness of an unmarked pit.

—William Maples on Czar Nicholas II

A favorite event at the annual conference of the American Academy of Forensic Science is the meeting of the "Last Word Society," where historic mysteries and murders are addressed and debated. Some of the topics that have been discussed in the past included: Who was Jack the Ripper? Did Butch Cassidy and the Sundance Kid die in Bolivia? Was Jesse James shot while hanging a picture? For scientists who are keen on solving puzzles, these historic questions, although not of medico-legal importance, hold a certain intrigue that cannot be ignored, and several forensic anthropologists have found themselves on forensic teams trying to answer yesterday's questions with today's technology.

Anastasia

Perhaps the most intriguing mystery of all surrounded Anastasia, the youngest daughter of the last czar of Russia. Her questionable disappearance sparked the creation of dozens of books and movies, as well as a flood of women who have claimed to be the royal daughter. Did Anastasia die along with her family, or could she have survived to live out her life in France or Florida? It is a question that many people have asked, and only science could answer.

In the middle of the night, July 16, 1918, Czar Nicholas II, his family, and a small group of servants were called to a basement room in the house where they were being held by Bolshevik soldiers. Under the pretense of having a photograph taken, the 11 prisoners were lined up, then subsequently shot by a firing squad. The bodies of the royal family were tossed onto a truck, taken to an abandoned mine shaft, and buried. Two days later, the local news announced the czar's death. There was no mention of his family.

Eight days after the murders, White Russian Army soldiers investigated the mine only to find 65 half-burned relics, including the czar's belt buckle, an emerald cross, a pearl earring, the empress's eyeglass case, military caps, shoe buckles, buttons, and an upper denture plate. The only human remain was a woman's severed finger.

Years passed, and the truth about the murders as well as the house where the assassinations were committed were bulldozed into oblivion. Because there was no official mention of the family's death, rumors began to spring up about the existence of members of the royal family who had slipped away unharmed. Many women and men have claimed to be one of the missing children. In the 1920s, a woman who had been suffering from amnesia surfaced in Berlin. She bore a striking resemblance to Anastasia and called herself Anna Anderson. She spent her whole life trying to prove her royal connection, but she died in 1984 no closer to her goal.

In the late 1980s, Mikhail Gorbachev declassified thousands of once secret Russian documents, including a report about the events surrounding the Czar's murder written by the chief assassin, Jacob Yurovsky. For the first time, it was made clear that the entire family, including a cook, footman, maid, and family physician, were gunned down. The report described multiple shots fired, but the women had stuffed jewels into their corsets, stopping the bullets. The soldiers struck them with their bayonets and hit them with their rifles before the women succumbed. The bodies were then taken to the Four Brothers Mine, stripped of their clothing, and dumped into an empty shaft, followed by hand grenades that exploded and sealed the hole.

But reports also described how three days later the soldiers returned to the mine, dug up the remains, and moved them to prevent the White

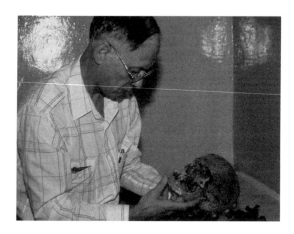

Forensic anthropologist
William Maples examines
the skull of Czar Nicholas
II. (© William R. Maples
Dead Men Do Tell Tales Dou-
bleday, 1994, courtesy of
Margaret Maples Gilliland)

Russian Army from finding the czar's body. The final resting place for the royal family was described as a bog close to a railroad crossing. There, two of the badly decomposing bodies were burned, and the rest were thrown into a pit measuring 6 feet deep and 8 feet wide. "The bodies were doused with sulfuric acid so they couldn't be recognized and to prevent any stink from them rotting. We scattered it with dirt and lime, put boards on top and rode over it several times—no trace of the hole remained," Yurovsky wrote.

The grave was eventually found, but the news was not made public until several years later in 1989. In 1992, forensic anthropologist William Maples was granted permission by the Russian government to examine the remains. Within months, a forensic crew consisting of forensic dentist Dr. Lowell Levine, pathologist Michael Baden, a hair and fiber analyst, Cathryn Oakes, and others were standing in a small room in the Russian Forensic–Medical Examination Bureau, surrounded by nine skeletons. The first day, the team managed to determine the general descriptions of each set of remains, but it took days to determine their identities.

All of the remains had fractured faces consistent with the accounts of being rammed with rifle butts, and all had signs of gunshot wounds. Each set of remains also revealed something unique about its owner. Body number 1 was that of a mature female. Her teeth had extensive, yet low quality dental work. Her ankle joints showed signs of extension, typical of someone who had spent a lifetime crouching or kneeling. This was the maid, Anna Demidova.

Body number 2 was that of a mature male with no upper teeth, which was consistent with the knowledge that Dr. Sergei Botkin had an upper dental plate, perhaps the same one that had been found 70 years before at the Four Brothers mine shaft. The skull's sloping forehead also was characteristic of the photographs of the family's personal physician.

Body number 3 was identified as the czar's daughter Olga. The bones were that of a young adult female in her mid-20s, fully grown as indicated by the roots of her third molars, or wisdom teeth. The bulging forehead and shape of the skull matched antemortem portraits of the young grand duchess.

Body number 4 was that of a mature male who was short in stature. The hipbones were slightly deformed, which was consistent with someone who rode horses. The forensic team agreed that this was Czar Nicholas II, even though the dentition was badly decayed and showed no signs of proper dental care. Perhaps he had a fear of dentists. All other characteristics, the age estimate, the facial features, and the man's love of horseback riding matched.

Number 5 was another young female. Her sacrum was not fully formed, and the roots of her wisdom teeth were incomplete, indicating that she was only in her mid-to-late teens at the time of death. This was Marie, who was 19 years old.

Body number 6 was also a young adult female whose growth patterns fell in between those of number 3 and number 5. This was Tatiana, who was 21 years old when she was killed with at least one shot to the back of her head.

If anyone had doubts that these remains were the royal family, then skeleton number 7 made it clear. The entire forensic team was awed by the elegant dental work made of gold, porcelain, and rare platinum gleaming from inside number 7's skull. The remains were of a mature women of wealth, the Czarina Alexandra, who had mentioned numerous visits to her dentist in her daily journals.

Skeleton number 8 was extremely fragmentary with severe acid damage to the bones, but still revealed to be of a man in his late 40s or 50s. By process of elimination, this was identified as the cook, Ivan Mikhailovich Kharitonov. The last set of remains, number 9, was a large, heavily built man and identified as the czar's trusted footman, Alexei Igorevich Trupp.

The nine sets of remains closed the book on nine members of the royal household, but still left questions regarding the two youngest children, 14-year-old Alexei and 17-year-old Anastasia. It has been suggested that the two people initially burned near the railroad crossing were the children, and that nothing short of a full-scale excavation of the entire site and the discovery of charred remains will complete the story of Anastasia.

Graveyard Detectives

Over the past 10 years there have been a series of historic cases reexamined in large part due to one man, James Starrs, professor of forensics at George Washington University. Although not a forensic anthropologist himself, he has routinely gathered top specialists in the forensic arena to shed new life on old cases. His first case took him to Colorado where he, along with forensic anthropologist Dr. Walter Birkby, excavated the mass grave of five victims thought to have been cannibalized by Alfred Packer in the 1870s.

In November 1873, Packer and 21 other prospectors headed out of Utah bound for Colorado, but by February, the group became snowbound and ran out of provisions. Alfred Packer and five others volunteered to go for help, but two months later Packer emerged alone and in pretty good shape for someone who had run out of food and nearly froze to death. Although he told several different versions of the events in the mountains, Packer finally settled on one account. Trapped without food, his companions died one by one, and those remaining ate the bodies in order to survive. He alone lasted until the weather turned and he was able to walk out. In the spring, a search party found the bodies of the five men lying on what is now called Cannibal Plateau. They were buried in a communal grave and Packer was sentenced to jail.

People in Colorado have long since speculated about Packer's winter diet, but Starrs wondered if he could answer the question once and for all. Did Packer really eat his companions? In 1989, Starrs and a team of anthropologists exhumed the bodies of the five men and carefully examined them for age, height, race, and gender and then examined them for signs of trauma. Birkby recorded many cut marks consistent with the process of removing flesh, as well as defense wounds to the arms and hands. "Clearly the bones were defleshed by one knife," Starrs said. "Packer was the only survivor and had the knife on him when he was found."

In order to *exhume* a body, Starrs has to get permission from the deceased's family or secure a court order. Not everyone is happy to cooperate. Starrs wanted to exhume Andrew and Abby Borden to see if in 1892 Lizzie Borden really did take an ax and give her mother 40 whacks, but was denied permission to exhume the bodies. He has also been denied access to documents pertaining to the death of former FBI director J. Edgar Hoover. But Starrs does not give up so easily. He has investigated the murders committed by the Boston Strangler, the death of Louisiana governor Huey Long, the mysterious suicide of CIA agent Frank Olsen, and in 1995, Starrs assembled forensic specialists to exhume and examine the alleged body of outlaw Jesse James, who was reportedly killed in 1882 while straightening a picture on the wall. Or was he? Some people believe that James escaped again and lived in Texas until he died of natural causes in 1942.

For this project Starrs sought the cooperation of the county medical examiner, three forensic anthropologists, a firearms expert, computer animator, document analyst, forensic geophysicist, two forensic molecular biologists, a forensic odontologist, forensic pathologist, forensic radiographer, toxicologist, and photographer.

The forensic anthropologists assisted in the exhumation and recovery of the remains from a grave in Mount Olivet Cemetery, Kearney, Missouri, and conducted the preliminary skeletal inventory. The remains were fragmentary and several bones were missing, but they were taken to the forensic lab where the anthropologists created a biological profile including age, stature, race, and time of death, which matched up with historically known attributes of the outlaw. Finally a mtDNA test was conducted using genetic material from the interior of two teeth. The profile matched similar tests taken for two known great-grandchildren.

Many forensic anthropologists think there should be limits and controls placed on who gets to exhume the dead and for what purpose. In the future, a panel of experts may be established to set down guidelines for exhumations and testing. Bodies would be reexamined only for reasons of great importance rather than idle curiosity. Even Starrs admits that there has to be substantial controversy surrounding the cause of death or identity of the deceased, as well as reason to think that current technology could help resolve it. For example, Starrs's investigation into the case of CIA agent Frank Olsen, who allegedly committed suicide by jumping out of a hotel window in 1953, did not provide solutions but created enough unsettling questions to force the New York district attorney to reopen the case.

Is there anyone that Starrs would not exhume? Yes. He, like many other forensic experts, would not exhume John F. Kennedy. Not only would there be little to learn from the examination, but Starrs says, it would be like exhuming his father. That's not to say that all presidents are exempt from seeing the light of day again. In 1991, William Maples participated in the exhumation of the nation's 12th president, Zachary

Taylor. For many years, there had been some controversy over his death. Historically he is said to have died from a bout of vomiting, abdominal spasms, and diarrhea that came on suddenly after eating a large meal of raw vegetables, fresh cherries, and iced buttermilk. He died within a week. But there has always been a quiet conspiracy theory that claimed the president had been poisoned with arsenic.

If this were true, then arsenic, like other metallic poisons, would be quickly deposited in the hair and bones of the victim. If the person lives a few days, as Taylor did, then the metals would remain in the victim forever.

In 1991, the Taylor family granted Maple's permission and the former president's body was removed from its crypt and taken to the state medical examiner's office where they took samples of hair and fingernails. Although there was much fanfare and media attention, the results seemed anticlimactic to the public. The tests came back negative. There was no evidence that Zachary Taylor was poisoned with arsenic.

The Angel of Death

Josef Mengele was a medical doctor and a high-ranking Nazi officer in Adolf Hitler's army during World War II. To many he is also known as the "Angel of Death," because Mengele was responsible for the deaths of more than 400,000 people at Auschwitz, the largest death camp in the Nazi regime. At Auschwitz, Mengele performed ghoulish tortures on the inmates, experimenting on them to prove his twisted theories of the superiority of the Aryan race.

On January 27, 1945, when the Russian army marched into Auschwitz, they found the camp empty of life. All that was left were smoldering furnaces and thousands of dead bodies. The Angel of Death had slipped away and vanished, and the search for the most wanted war criminal began.

Nazi hunters followed every lead and checked every rumor, tracking Mengele across countries and over continents, and each time they came up empty. For 40 years after the liberation of Auschwitz, the search continued. In 1985, a new clue surfaced that led Nazi hunters to a grave in the hills of Embú, Brazil, and a woman named Lisolette Bossert. Bossert told the police that in 1979 she had arranged for the burial of a friend named Wolfgang Gerhard and that Gerhard had drowned in a swimming accident. But after hours of interrogation, Bossert admitted that the man in the grave was not Gerhard but Mengele. Wolfgang Gerhard had really been an Austrian and a friend to both Bossert and Mengele. In 1971, Gerhard had decided to return to Austria, but before he did, he gave Mengele his Brazilian identification card. Mengele's photograph was inserted onto it, giving him a new identity. Prior to that he had used the name Peter Hochbichler. It was believed that Mengele had been found.

The discovery of Josef Mengele was of worldwide importance. He was a major war criminal, and if he was still alive he could be tried for his crimes against humanity. And if he was dead, many people could put their minds to rest knowing that the mystery was over.

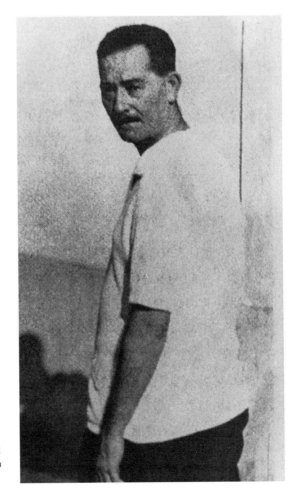

Skeletal analysis from an international team of forensic scientists determined that Mengele died in Brazil in 1979. [Library of Congress]

Quickly news of the discovery spread. The governments of Brazil, the United States, and West Germany sent teams of forensic scientists to São Paulo, Brazil, to study the remains. An independent team from the Wiesenthal Center in California, acting on behalf of many Jewish Americans, was also sent. One of the top forensic anthropologists, Clyde Snow, was on the team.

The body (called the Embú skeleton) had two possible identities. It could not yet be ruled out that Bossert's story was another attempt to throw authorities off Mengele's track. The possibility that the skeleton could be Gerhard's had to be checked too. Before looking at the bones, the first item of business was gathering information about the physical characteristics of Gerhard from medical and governmental records and of Mengele from German secret service reports, dental charts, photographs, and personal interviews. This information would be compared to the skeletal data.

Next, each forensic team got to look at the remains, each scientist pouring over them, attacking the project from his own specialty. The skull had been badly smashed by a grave digger's shovel, and many of the pieces were no bigger than a dime. It would have to be reconstructed. German anthropologist Richard Helmer, a skull expert, took on the job. The rest of the teams took turns measuring and analyzing the various bones.

The first question to be answered was whether the skeleton was male or female. The head of the femur, and the head of the humerus were large, the jaw was square and robust, and the pelvis narrow. The experts all agreed that the Embú skeleton was that of a male.

After several days, Helmer was finished with the skull reconstruction. The shape of the face indicated that the man was Caucasian. Snow measured the femur to estimate the man's height. When the man was alive he stood 173.5 centimeters, or 5 feet 8 inches tall. That ruled out the real Gerhard. Information collected on Gerhard indicated that he was taller. In fact, Gerhard had a German nickname, Langer. In the United States he would have been called Stretch. According to the German S.S. reports, Mengele was 174 centimeters tall.

The bones were from a man between 60 and 70 years old. Information on Gerhard indicated that he was only 50 when he died. Dr. Ellis Kerley, who devised the microscopic bone analysis for determining age, sliced a wafer-thin section of the femur. Under the microscope he determined that the man had died in his late 60s.

From the shoulder blade and shoulder socket, scientists discovered that the Embú skeleton had been right-handed. Mengele was right-handed, but so are most people. So far the teams had found nothing that refuted the possibility that the man in the grave was Josef Mengele, but they still did not have conclusive proof.

X rays taken of Mengele before he died would have been very useful. They are like fingerprints; no two people's X rays are alike. But there were no dental X rays to be found. Mengele was believed to have lived in Brazil for many years, and the teeth on the skeleton showed signs of dental work. There had to have been a dentist somewhere who had worked on those teeth.

Meanwhile, Helmer, who in Germany had perfected the technique of video imaging a photograph on a skull, was ready to compare the skull with a photograph of Mengele. If the skull was indeed that of Josef Mengele, it would match up with the photograph point by point. If it did not, then it was somebody else buried in that grave. Helmer stuck markers on the skull to correspond with the known tissue thicknesses. Then he focused a video camera on the skull, and one on a photograph of Mengele in his Nazi uniform. The forensic teams were gathered together in the photography room, all eyes fixed on the monitor where the image of Mengele appeared and then the ghostly image of the skull appeared beneath it. Each marker seemed to touch the filmy image of the skin as if it was holding it up from inside. Every point matched.

The image convinced everyone in the room that the man in the grave was indeed Mengele—but that was not good enough for the rest of the world. The team's responsibility was to use physical evidence to prove beyond any doubt the identity of the man. The forensic team needed to find antemortem dental X rays.

After more searching and interviews, a dentist in a distant Brazilian village admitted to having a patient in 1978 named Gerhard. Pointing him out in a photograph, the dentist pointed directly to Mengele, then handed over the much-needed dental X rays. The antemortem X rays were superimposed with X rays taken of the teeth in the Embú skull. If the Gerhard X rays matched the skull, then it would prove that the man who called himself Gerhard in 1978 had really been Josef Mengele. The X rays matched perfectly right down to the gap between the two front teeth, which was one of Mengele's more striking features.

Each team felt that they had proven without a doubt that the body in the grave was Josef Mengele, who had been living quietly in Brazil under an assumed identity of Wolfgang Gerhard. For the Brazilian, U.S., and German governments and the Wiesenthal team, the case of the most wanted murderer was closed.

OLD BONES

They were in fact very much like us.

—Christian Fischer, Silkeborg Museum, Denmark

Most forensic anthropologists are not full-time specialists. They are primarily curators at museums or professors at universities, concentrating on ancient mysteries dug from the ground of archaeological sites, only occasionally called upon to examine fresher remains. But there is a lot of crossover in their two passions. "We apply what we learn from archaeological excavations to criminal cases, and vice versa," says Douglas Owsley. "The information flows both ways." For example, Owsley's experience working with prehistoric war victims who were dismembered immediately after death proved invaluable when he was called upon to examine hundreds of bone fragments from the 1991 case of serial killer Jeffrey Dahmer. Owsley had to examine each fragment for signs of cut marks and determine the age and sex of the victim whose bones Dahmer had crushed with a heavy tool and scattered over two acres.

While working on a forensic case, anthropologists bring all they know about the variations of the human skeleton to define one specific individual. But when they look at historic or prehistoric remains, anthropologists ask themselves, "What does this individual say about an entire population or period of time?" In forensics, the focus is on the individual, while in archaeology, the focus is on population and variation—variation through time, across geography, genders, ages, and socioeconomic classes. The questions may be different, but the same skills and techniques apply. Scientists assess the sex, age, race, and stature of the remains and look for signs of trauma and disease.

The study of human remains from the past has been called archaeological skeletal biology, osteoarchaeology, as well as zooarchaeology, but many practitioners accept the term bioarchaeology. Like its forensic counterpart, it is a multidisciplinary field blending archaeological recovery methods and physical anthropological analysis. Their study of large populations of ancient remains has cast new light on old theories and long held beliefs. For example, it was once widely thought that the shift from a foraging way of life to the practice of agriculture was an improvement in ancient man's lifestyle. Archaeologists discovered the evidence of great cities and civilizations around the globe, but bioarchaeologists uncovered osteological evidence suggesting that there was also a great cost associated with this lifestyle change. The bones of early farmers showed signs that they suffered from more disease, malnutrition, infection, and increased physical labor compared to their foraging forefathers. A similar impact on the human body also resulted from other major changes, such as the colonization of the New World. Both the colonists and Native American populations suffered great physical hardships.

Ancient bones speak of hard lives—arthritis, fractures, sickness, heavy labor, fatal wounds, and war. But those who were wounded were often treated and healed. Those who were deformed were fed and sheltered. Their bones hint at strong bodies and varied diets, of pregnancies and growth, of families and caring. They were a lot like us. Although the data provided by hundreds of nameless skeletons from the past reveals truths about our history, it is the story revealed by a single intact body like a mummy that sparks the public's interest in the past.

Mummies

Mummies present a dilemma for anthropologists who, in a forensic setting, clean the bones before conducting their exam. Although it was common for scientists, as well as wealthy Victorians a hundred years ago, to unwrap mummies, it is no longer the practice. Today, anthropologists use other methods borrowed from modern medicine to "see" inside the linens without damaging the body.

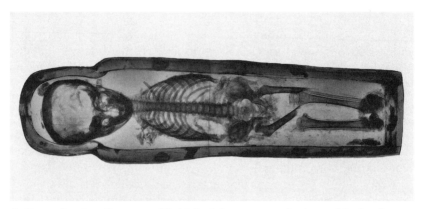

An X ray of an Egyptian mummified infant shows a curved spine and broken legs.
[The Field Museum, Neg. # C5A59105]

Simple X rays have revealed more than one individual in a coffin or animal remains inside a coffin where human remains were expected to be. A radiograph taken of the head of Egyptian pharaoh Ramses II revealed for the first time a tiny animal bone placed inside the nose and behind it a cluster of beads.

Scientists can get an even more detailed look using CAT scans. Many of the mummies that are housed in American museums have made at least one visit to a nearby hospital. In 1998, Kevin Smith, associate curator of anthropology at the Buffalo Museum of Science, arranged to have the mummy of Nes-min CAT scanned at Buffalo General Hospital. "The doctors loved him," Smith said. "Nes-min didn't squirm or fidget." Because the mummy was already dead, the technicians could bombard it with much more radiation than they could a living patient, which resulted in images with incredibly high resolution. The CAT scan machine uses X rays to take cross-sectional axial images, or "slices," of the body as it is passed through the tire-shaped scanner. Each slice was made in increments as small as 1.5 millimeters with a scanned diameter of 3.2 millimeters, giving doctors unusually detailed coverage that even showed the grain and construction of the wooden coffin and the layers of resin as it was poured over the body a little at a time. When the scan was completed, researchers then reassembled the slices on a computer screen to create a three-dimensional model. A 3-D processing or graphics workstation, similar to those used to create high quality computerized special effects for movies, allows researchers to "see" the insides of a mummy in different ways. One way is to "fly" through the abdomen. A "fly" through of

Nes-min revealed the long incision in his side where his organs were removed, tightly rolled linens stuffed into his abdominal cavity to keep his shape, and small bundles of linen placed in his eye sockets.

From the hieroglyphics on the coffin, Smith knew that Nes-min had been a priest in the temple of Min in the ancient city of Khent-min in the fifth century B.C. "The coffin text is equivalent to a modern-day résumé with references," Smith said. "Besides prayers, the deceased's name, and list of ancestors, it also tells the person's occupation and good deeds." However, the coffin text did not tell Smith what Nes-min's life was really like. Smith assumed that Nes-min's life as a priest would have been one of ease, but Nes-min's bones revealed the opposite. Nes-min was 40 to 45 years old when he died. He had an abscess in his jaw and badly worn teeth, a common occurrence in a land where sand permeates everything including food. At one time in his life, he must have experienced a severe blow to his back, which broke several ribs. He survived and his ribs healed, although badly. Tiny lines across the ends of Nes-min's long bones, called Harris lines, told Smith that as a teen Nes-min had suffered several periods when his growth stopped then started again, perhaps due to malnutrition or sickness. One of his vertebrae had collapsed, suggesting that throughout his life Nes-min may have performed heavy physical labor or the damage could have occurred in the accident or attack that broke his ribs. And even after death his body had been handled roughly. The CAT scan showed fractures across both femurs—once thought to be antemortem trauma—which radiated out through the linens as well, indicating that they occurred after death.

Otzi

Not all mummies are man-made, many are created by nature. Extreme weather conditions, such as the dry heat of a desert or the freezing effect of the Arctic, stop decomposition and preserve tissue for millennia. One of the more celebrated and surprising examples was a body found in the Oetz Valley along the Austrian-Italian border in the Alps on September 19, 1991.

Every spring, the melting snow reveals the remains of unfortunate hikers who lost their lives the previous winter, and by September of 1991, forensic expert Rainer Henn of the Innsbruck Forensic Institute had already dealt with six bodies found that year. The first two were mountain guides who disappeared in 1953; the third, a guide who lost his way in 1981; and the last two were hikers who had been reported missing in 1934—so old bodies were nothing new. But the sixth body proved to be different. It was dark and leathery and fully preserved by natural freeze-drying effects of the wind and cold. It took 30 men using pickaxes and compressors to free the man from the ice. Once free, Henn realized that this man was special. Anthropologists determined that the man in the ice had been frozen for more than 5,000 years.

The iceman, nicknamed Otzi, has been given a permanent home in the South Tyrol Museum of Archaeology in Bolzano, Italy. Except for a brief period when he was allowed to thaw so scientists could conduct tests, Otzi is kept in a frozen state at -6 degrees centigrade, the same temperature as the glacier that preserved him for so long. Over the past 10 years, more than 150 specialists have examined his skin, hair, bones, stomach contents, clothing, possessions, and more. Otzi's skin was so hard it took a saw, not a scalpel, to cut off small pieces of tissue for analysis. X rays of the head revealed the sutures in the skull, which gave an age estimate of 35 to 40 years. Otzi once stood 5 feet 3 inches tall, weighed only 110 pounds, and had dark hair and a full beard. But what did his face look like?

By using a CAT scan of his head, scientists created an exact copy of Otzi's skull. A model was made by passing an ultraviolet laser beam over the surface of a vat of photosensitive liquid plastic, which quickly hardened under the beam. The CAT scan images dictated where the laser was directed. After each pass of the laser beam, the mass of hardened plastic was sunk deeper into the vat, gradually taking on a three-dimensional form, one slice at a time. The model skull was then used to reconstruct Otzi's face, which was partially destroyed from the movement of the glacier.

Otzi's teeth were cavity free, but worn down by the grinding action of eating a gritty diet of coarse-ground grain. Further chemical tests, including one called stable-isotope analysis, indicated that Otzi may have been a vegetarian or even a vegan. A stable isotope is an identifiable form of a chemical element, which is not subject to radioactive decay. The isotope nitrogen-15, for example, can be differentiated from nitrogen-14 because it has one more neutron. Chemists can determine how much of a particular isotope is present by measuring this minute difference in mass. Different environments have different isotope signatures, and the isotopic ratio of a particular area circulates through the food chain. It is absorbed and preserved by plants, then carried to and altered by animals that eat the plants. So, testing the amount of specific isotopes present in Otzi's 5,000-year-old hair and fingernails told researchers that he ate nothing but plant material the month before he died. His isotopic ratio was consistent with modern vegans.

A grooved earlobe suggests he wore an earring, and a series of strange tattoos that were found on the top of the left foot, across the kneecap, and running down the small of his back may have been placed there as some sort of folk medicine. Many cultures today place similar black-lined tattoos on parts of the body that ache, believing that they will cure the ailment. To test this hypothesis, X rays were taken of Otzi's spine, knee, ankles, and feet and revealed degenerative wear and tear that might have been painful. So it seems reasonable to suggest that the iceman placed tattoos on those spots, believing they would heal the pain.

Earlier in his life, Otzi had broken five ribs, which all healed well, but just before he died, his left arm was broken above the elbow and four ribs were cracked. For nearly 10 years, researchers thought Otzi died after a fall or becoming lost in a storm or that he just froze to death on top of a mountain, but now they think it could have been murder. Radiologist Paul Gostner identified a small one-half-inch (2-centimeter) long slate arrowhead embedded 2 to 3 inches (5–7 cm) deep in Otzi's left shoulder. Gostner was able to follow the path of the projectile through the bones and pieced together what happened. The arrowhead shattered the scapula, tearing through nerves and major blood vessels. It would have paralyzed Otzi's left arm. Gostner and other forensic experts suggest that he would have bled to death within 10 hours, prompting a new question, "Who shot Otzi?"

Since the discovery of Otzi in the Alps, many other bodies have been uncovered that pose even more ponderous questions. Caucasian-looking mummies found in the northwest province of Xinjiang, China, have prompted a controversy over the accepted timeline of when East met West. Some scientists suggest that Cherchen Man—the mummy that stands almost 6 feet tall and sports ginger-colored hair over a narrow face, pale skin, high cheekbones, and long nose—indicates that Europeans were interacting with Asian communities several hundred years earlier than previously thought.

The Body in the Bog

Some of the more mysterious bodies ever found are those cut from the thick mire of European peat bogs. One of the most studied is the 2,000-year-old body called Lindow Man, dredged from the peat bogs of Lindow Moss in northwest England. Although the lower half of the body is missing, it is obviously that of a man because of its well-preserved beard, mustache, and sideburns. It is also apparent that he died a violent death. Lindow Man had been struck on the back of the head at least twice by a narrow-bladed weapon similar to a hatchet, which cut the skin and fractured the skull. He suffered severe blows to his back and chest, which broke a rib and other bones. After he was unconscious, a knotted rope of sinew was tied around his neck, strangling him. Finally his throat was slit, severing the jugular vein, and his lifeless body was dropped into the peat bog.

Lindow Man was in his mid-20s when he died, stood about 5 feet 6 inches tall, and weighed about 130 pounds. He suffered mild arthritis in his lower back and had excellent teeth. His intestines were riddled with parasitic worm eggs, and his stomach contents revealed a last meal of charred unleavened bread or griddle cake and a small quantity of mistletoe, a toxic plant associated with the Druids.

Lindow Man's preserved remains reveal a violent death from stab wounds, slit throat, broken bones, and strangulation.
[British Museum]

A fiberoptic endoscope—a miniature camera with a light source mounted on small flexible tubing—was inserted into Lindow Man's skull and showed that the brain, which appeared to be present on CAT scans, had deteriorated to a mass of puttylike tissue.

We know what happened to Lindow Man, but we do not know why. Was he sacrificed or executed for a crime? We do know that he is not unique. Many other bodies have been found since the 1940s, when people of northwestern Europe began using peat as fuel, making some startling discoveries as they carved huge blocks of peat from the bogs. Most of the time they were thought to be recent remains because they were so well preserved by the extremely moist and acidic conditions of the bog, which deters bacterial decomposition and turns a corpse's skin to leather. But the bodies were more than 2,000 years old, belonging to a time dominated by Germanic tribes of the Iron Age. Most of the victims were hung with the ropes left wrapped around their necks, hit over the head, or stabbed. Some suffered broken bones, slit throats, and crushed skulls. A number of the women had one side of their heads shaved, a sign of disgrace in medieval times. Others were treated more gently and were placed in prepared graves in the bogs rather than being tossed in. Although these bodies offer so many mysteries and so much information, they are also a subject of concern. Who keeps them? Are they displayed, and if they are how are they displayed? This concern crops up every time human remains are unearthed.

The Repatriation Act

Stanley Rhine in his book *Bone Voyage* points to one of forensic anthropology's perennial problems—fixing on a definition. "One measure of whether a skeleton can be said to be of medico-legal interest is if the person analyzing it may have to go to court to testify on his or her findings," he wrote. He was referring to cases where the perpetrator of a murder might still be alive and held accountable for his or her actions, but that aspect of forensic work may have taken on a much older clientele—that of ancient Native American remains that are being repatriated, or returned to their people.

In 1990, the federal government passed a controversial law called the Native American Graves Protection and Repatriation Act (NAGPRA), which came in response to decades of hard feelings and disputes. Archaeologists have routinely excavated and removed ancient remains, viewing them as an invaluable source of information about the past, to be studied and stored in museums and universities. But Native Americans have viewed this practice as the desecration of their sacred burial grounds and the uprooting of their ancestors. These opposing views have caused many states to enact laws governing the handling of ancient remains uncovered by construction or archaeological excavation. When a burial is unearthed, the local Native American community leaders are notified and participate in the decisions that are made concerning the site. Native American leaders have realized that it is better to have archaeologists remove the skeletons intact rather than have a bulldozer come and destroy them. The bones must be examined in order to determine if they are ancient Native American remains or not. At sites where the remains are not immediately threatened by construction, the remains can be studied in place and covered again.

NAGPRA, however, calls for the return, upon request, of all Native American remains and artifacts currently housed in institutions receiving federal funding. In order to comply with the law, the Smithsonian, for example, established its Repatriation Office in the Anthropology Department in the fall of 1991. Its team of osteologists, skeletal biologists, dentists, radiographers, and photographers have so far documented more than half of its collection of more than 16,000 sets of Native American remains.

The first step was to inventory their collection and make that information available to Native American communities by 1995. It has been a lengthy process and disputes that arise are mediated by a federal panel of experts. Each set of remains is examined and assessed for age at death and gender, as well as the condition of the bones. This description is not only for the Smithsonian's own records, but also to help in the repatriation effort. Some Native American groups, for example, have different burial procedures for men and women, and young and old. The condition of the remains, such as weathering or staining, tells a lot about its original location and manner of burial. The Dakotas, for instance, built mounds, and Ojibwe buried certain artifacts with their dead.

The team describes and measures the morphology of the bones and, in particular, the face to help determine ancestry. Many of the ancient Native American remains also show signs of culturally related modifications. Infants that were carried on a cradleboard developed a flattening of the back of the head, and the practice of lip ornamentation often left a person with altered dentition and jawbone.

For fairly recent remains, it is easy to determine tribal affiliation, because documentation or archaeologist's field notes accompany the remains. Coupling that with what is known about early tribal migratory patterns, researchers can make a fairly accurate decision as to cultural affiliation.

Each museum and state has set up a system to handle the job. In Minnesota, for example, all repatriated human remains pass through the Hamline University Osteology Lab so that osteologists can extract any final scientific data from them before they are reburied. But as one researcher said, it is unfortunate that these remains will not be available later, because techniques are always being improved, and new technologies may be developed that could reveal even more from the remains.

Kennewick Man

But can a set of bones be assigned tribal affiliation definitively? Some bones pose more problems than others and remain locked up in storage and in court. One skeleton that is likely to remain in a closet for some time until a judge determines its future was dubbed Kennewick Man. It was discovered on July 28, 1996, by two college students who were watching boat races from the banks of the Columbia River in Kennewick, Washington. They took the skull to the county coroner who called Jim Chatters, an anthropologist who consulted for the county on forensic cases. Chatters and a police crew returned to the riverbed and uncovered most of a complete skeleton. The only parts that were missing were the sternum and a few small bones of the hands and feet.

Chatters gave the remains a standard forensic exam, even though he knew they were old. But there were two incongruous features. The face lacked the definitive Native American characteristics typically found in ancient remains of that region. The face was narrow and prognathous rather than broad and flat. Perhaps this was an early settler? X rays revealed the second striking feature. Embedded in the right pelvis was a leaf-shaped, serrated projectile point commonly used more than 8,000 years ago. These two features startled everyone who worked on the remains, and forced the county coroner to call for a radiocarbon date, which placed the man living and breathing more than 9,000 years ago. Instantly, it raised questions in the academic community about the accepted theories of who the first people of the New World were. Was this Caucasian-looking skeleton a fluke, or did it point to more serious concerns as to the origin of the first humans on this continent?

Four days after the radiocarbon results were announced, the Army Corps of Engineers, who were in charge of the remains, decided to return them back to an alliance of five tribes—the Umatilla, Yakama, Nez Perce, Wanapum, and Colville. Following that decision, a group of eight anthropologists filed a lawsuit to stop the internment so that more studies could be carried out. Shortly after, a European religious group called Asatru Folk Assembly also filed suit, asking for the opportunity to determine if Kennewick Man was one of their ancestors. Three years later, a Samoan chieftain requested the right to make a claim on the remains but was denied by the U.S. magistrate judge John Jelderks.

The situation did not improve when in 1998 pieces of Kennewick Man's femurs were reported missing by the Army Corps of Engineers. They were found three years later tucked away in the sheriff's office evidence bunker. Like any good forensic case, chain of custody for evidence must be documented and maintained. This lapse may raise its ugly head if DNA testing is ever performed, because contamination of DNA from those who have handled the bones might lead to an inaccurate genetic profile. But as of September 2001, the judge had made no final decision regarding Kennewick Man, who remains locked away.

Before Kennewick Man was put away, forensic scientists were able to reveal a lot about the 9,000-year-old man. When he was a young man, perhaps only a teenager, a thin, sharp stone projectile point hit him with such force that it became embedded in his hip. Without help, Kennewick Man might have died, but he survived. His wound healed and the pelvic bone grew and molded completely around the projectile point. He grew to be a robust, healthy man and lived 45 to 55 years. Although researchers try to piece together this individual's life history, Chatters points out there is much we will never be able to know. "No matter how long we might study the Kennewick Man we would never know the form or color of his eyes, skin, and hair, whether his hair was curly or straight, his lips thin or full—in short many of the characteristics by which we judge living people's racial affiliation," wrote Chatters. "We will never be certain if his wound was by accident or intent, what language he spoke, or his religious beliefs. We cannot know if he is truly anyone's ancestor."

SILENT WITNESS

. . . One corner of the world can no longer slaughter its people while the other corner goes on about its business.

—Karen Ramey Burns, University of North Carolina

Over the past 20 years, the role of forensic anthropology has grown in focus and scope. It no longer focuses solely on bare-bone skeletons but includes the analysis of remains that are partially decomposed, mummified, dismembered, or burned and now reaches beyond local jurisdictions, across national borders to encompass not only crimes against an individual but crimes against humanity.

A Grave at Ovcara

Prior to the war of 1991 in Yugoslavia, Ovcara was a state-run farm on the outskirts of the Croatian city of Vukovar. During the war it became a mass grave, and after the war it was an international crime scene. In 1996, forensic anthropologist William Haglund and a team of international forensic investigators were authorized by the United Nations to exhume more than 200 bodies that were thought to be buried at Ovcara. The work atmosphere was far from a normal forensic situation. Razor wire fencing ran the perimeter of the site, and armed Jordanian guards stood atop an armored personnel carrier. A portable refrigerator unit stood in for the sterile white morgue, and rooms in an abandoned factory building were outfitted into autopsy suites.

The workers had to gently tug each corpse free of the entangling limbs of the bodies around it and describe each one in a running monologue before placing it in a bag with a label. This physical evidence would be used against the perpetrators of some of the worst war crimes of the century and would hopefully corroborate the story of a wounded soldier from Vukovar who, a year earlier, told his horror story to anthropologist Clyde Snow.

Until 1991, Yugoslavia lived up to the meaning of its name "united Slavs." It was a country of six republics (Croatia, Serbia, Bosnia and Hercegovina, Montenegro, Macedonia, Slovenia) and two independent provinces welded together by Marshall Tito after World War II. It was an ethnic quilt of Muslims, Serbs, and Croats living in relative peace as neighbors and friends until 1987, when Serbian nationalist feelings emerged under Slobodan Milosevic. This incited the formation of other ultranationalist parties, and in 1991 Croatia and Slovenia declared their independence. Milosevic responded with brute force, and the Yugoslav National Army descended on Croatia. The residents of Vukovar suffered three months of artillery, rocket, and aircraft fire, defending themselves with only a ragtag army of 1,800 volunteers, including Snow's informant who described this event.

He had been injured during battle and lay on a mattress on the floor in Vukovar Hospital. Wounded soldiers and civilians lined the corridors, rested in the basement, and convalesced on the patio. While the soldier was in the hospital, troops stormed the city, taking over the hospital as well as other major sites. The Serb commanding officer promised patients that they would be released unharmed, but that promise was not kept. Instead, injured soldiers and hospital workers were forced onto six military buses and driven out of the city to a large building on Ovcara farm, where they were taunted and beaten with rifle butts. The soldier told Snow that every 15 minutes or so he noticed small groups of 20 men were being loaded onto another truck and taken away. The sun had gone down by the time it was his turn, and he took his only chance for survival and jumped off the moving truck as it lurched over the rutted road. As he ran into the wheat field he heard the gunfire.

Four years later, as the bodies were pulled out of the Ovcara grave, it became clear that the soldier's story was true. Some of the bodies

Forensic investigators from the International Commission on Missing Persons exhume bones from a mass grave in Bosnia. (Courtesy of the International Commission on Missing Persons in the former Yugoslavia)

wore hospital smocks and white clogs typically worn by Croatian hospital staff. Others were bandaged or wore slings or casts on their arms and legs. A pair of crutches lay among the remains. One body even had a catheter dangling from its pelvis. Scattered along the northwest perimeter of the grave were more than 75 cartridge casings, and along the opposite bank, stood a row of acacia trees riddled with bullet holes, all the signs of an execution.

Haglund and his team excavated other sites in the former Yugoslavia too. One of the largest was a mass grave at Pilca farm that was 20 feet deep and more than 100 feet long. Thousands of other bodies were found in all states of decomposition along "the trail of life and death," a route taken by countless Muslim men who walked from the occupied war zones to Croat-held territory. To avoid capture the groups of men moved at night and hid in the woods and in abandoned buildings by day, keeping out of sight of Serb soldiers intent on killing them. Many did not survive the journey.

Thousands of bodies were found along the "trail of life and death." These remains were found among the leaf litter. [Courtesy of the International Commission on Missing Persons in the Former Yugoslavia]

Over the course of four years of forensic excavations, Haglund and his team mapped, photographed, and recorded each body, bone, and bullet. This information became the primary physical evidence presented to the International Criminals Tribunal set up by the United Nations Security Council. Convened in 1993, the tribunal was the first international criminal court since the Nuremberg and Tokyo trials of World War II.

Crimes against Humanity

Unfortunately, there does not seem to be a corner of the world that is not affected by major human-rights violations of one type or another. Most forensic anthropologists would agree that working any murder case is important, but the situation becomes more dire when the death toll rises into the thousands, when the perpetrator is a government, and when the victims are its citizens. It is an arduous task to prosecute the accused because there are so few survivors, and those who do survive are afraid to speak up. Historically, these atrocities were difficult to document—until now.

Forensic anthropology provides the world with the means to uncover the evidence the perpetrators thought was so well hidden. Human-rights exhumations not only provide the evidence against the nation or officials responsible for the crimes, but, more importantly, they bring closure and peace to families tortured by uncertainty. They also open the eyes of the rest of the world that silently looked the other way.

Thirty years ago, digging up the remains of victims of political crimes was a novel concept, but it took hold because there were few or no other avenues the victims' families could take to get the justice and peace of mind they sought. The first major human-rights exhumation project took place in the 1980s when Clyde Snow was invited to Argentina to help two groups called the Asociación Madres de Plaza de Mayo and Asociación Abuelas de Plaza de Mayo (Mothers and Grandmothers of the Plaza de Mayo) find and identify their children.

Argentina

The political climate in Argentina in the mid-1970s was unstable. Although Isabel Péron, the third wife of beloved leader Juan Péron, was president, she was unable to make needed social and economic improvements. Radical leftist groups, made up mostly of college students, fought against the government and one another for political control. Leftist groups, including radical Péronists and Monteneros, bombed government buildings as squads of soldiers and civilians armed with assault rifles patrolled the streets.

In 1976, the military seized power from Isabel Péron and set up a three-man military regime, or junta, on the pretext of leading the country back to democracy. But there was nothing democratic about the junta. It abolished the congress, all labor unions, and political parties. Speaking out against the government became punishable by imprisonment or death. During the seven years that the junta held power, more than 10,000 people were killed at the hands of police death squads.

Armed police raided homes in the middle of the night, yanked people out of bed and shot them, or arrested them and took them to secret detention camps, where they were horribly tortured, often in front of spouses, parents, or children. Whole families were taken and never heard from again. Pregnant women who gave birth in prison never saw their babies and believed they were given to military families or sold for adoption. Mothers and grandmothers protested and demanded information about their missing children. They wanted answers, but the government ignored them and retaliated against them as well.

But the largest group to suffer were the young college students who were members of the banned political parties. Sometimes the only "crime" they committed was socializing with someone thought to be a political activist. Cristina Costanzo was one of them. She was abducted at gunpoint early in the morning of October 14, 1976, along with seven of her friends. They were shoved into one of the black Fords that patrolled the street, collecting "political prisoners." Years later, Cristina's family learned that she had been put in prison that night, but her friends were not. The day after the abduction, seven bodies were found in a heap at the side of a dirt road at the edge of the city. Each had been shot once in the back of the head. These bodies were taken to the morgue and registered as N.N.—no name. Later that day, they were piled on a truck along with other dead, taken to a cemetery, and buried in a mass grave similar to many others all over the country.

The bloody military reign ended in 1983, when the Argentine government, defeated by the British in the war over the Falkland Islands (Islas Malvinas), disbanded and declared free elections. In 1984, efforts were under way to identify the dead. Argentineans clambered for information about their missing relatives, who became known as "the disappeared." That is when Snow, along with a group of anthropology students from Argentina University, showed the world how forensic identification methods could give mourning families a little peace. Dr. Snow taught students how to look at a set of bones and determine the age at death, gender from the pelvis, race from the skull, and help piece together broken lives like those of the Costanzo family.

In 1984, when the cemetery was opened, the students uncovered many of the bodies, put them in plastic bags, and took them to the morgue where Clyde Snow and forensic odontologist Lowell Levine were working. The small room they were assigned to was lined with the plastic garbage bags full of bones. Broken bags spilled out their contents on the dirty floor, where no one had bothered to pick them up.

Only one family had sent in information to help in identifying the remains. The Costanzos sent dental X rays taken one year before Cristina disappeared. Levine studied the X ray as Snow started to open the bags and pull out skulls. He lined them up on the long examining tables, grouping them by sex and age. They were interested in the group of skulls 20 to 30 years old, because they knew that Cristina was 25. Most of the skulls had gunshot wounds in them, some in the back of the head in a typical execution style. Snow fingered one skull that seemed to fit Cristina's description, but several teeth from the upper row had been lost during the exhumation. Fortunately, the lower jaw was intact and could be x-rayed. Comparing the two X rays, Levine showed Snow and the students that the fillings were a perfect match, and the root shape and bone pattern were identical. It was Cristina Costanzo. Hers was one of the first of many forensic anthropological identifications to be used in a court of law in Argentinean human-rights abuse cases.

Working a Mass Grave

The handling of human-rights cases has come a long way since Clyde Snow worked in Argentina, and most of the investigators working on these types of projects were trained either directly or indirectly by him. Over the years, Snow, Haglund, and others have develop new excavation procedures and created better forms for collecting antemortem data. But each project is a learning experience, and flexibility is key in working the various sites because of the terrain, type of burial, and cultural diversity between the investigators and the victims, as well as among the investigators themselves. Specialists working at the Pilca site, for example, came from the United States, Holland, Peru, Philippines, United Kingdom, Argentina, Chile, Guatemala, and Honduras. They are primarily volunteers—anthropologists, radiologists, odontologists, and police investigators—who may spend several weeks or months at a site, living in less than comfortable accommodations. In Bosnia, they slept in sleeping bags on bunks, waking at dawn to have military personnel escort them on a two-hour trip to the site. Haglund often slept in his jeep next to the pit, so there would be no dispute over the integrity of the site or any question about the chain of custody of the evidence.

There are three basic facets of human-rights work: interviewing family members for antemortem information, excavating the graves, and analyzing the remains. For each step, anthropologists are uniquely qualified. Their broad-based education in cultural diversity allows them the flexibility and sensitivity to deal with the vast cultural and linguistic differences that exist between themselves and the informants. Team members must interview the families of the missing to get as much antemortem medical information and document as many identifying characteristics as possible. But some characteristics, such as eye color, do not translate well. To address this discrepancy, anthropologists have developed color charts that allow family members to point to the color of their loved one's eyes or hair or clothing. To avoid any further errors, blank diagrams are also used to point out the location of tattoos and scars. The smallest detail is important because official antemortem medical records may be few or nonexistent in poor countries, and in these cases identifications have been made from as little as a handful of severely arthritic neck vertebra, the tip of a single finger, or a tumor on a big toe.

The forensic investigators have to also be aware of common burial practices so they can easily identify those that are suspicious. For example, in the United States, most bodies are buried fully clothed and facing up, but in Islamic countries, the dead are shrouded only in a sheet of cotton and placed on their side, facing Mecca. Knowing what's normal allows investigators to distinguish between criminal activity and a culturally acceptable burial.

Working in another country, the team also has to be sensitive to the political policies, religious practices, and local laws. Excavation crews must secure the permission of national or local government agencies, religious officials, and landowners, if necessary. In some parts of the world, government officials need to be present, in others a religious ceremony must precede the exhumation, and in other countries families should be invited.

Although part of the mission is to identify victims, the primary goal is to collect evidence. International tribunals are more concerned about documenting criminal acts rather than the identification of individuals. Sometimes, as in Bosnia, the identifications are left to local forensic experts to carry out, so the excavation crew can focus on documenting the violence and sequence of events. As a grave is exhumed, every bit of evidence, such as a bullet, ligature, or blindfold, is mapped. This is done using sophisticated electronic survey equipment. A metal pole is placed over an object, such as a bullet, and a laser beam is bounced off the mirrors on top of the pole back to the stationary transit, which automatically calculates the distance between the transit and the object.

This information is stored in an electronic notebook and entered into a computer program, which creates a 3-D map of the site. It can take half a day to excavate with trowels and brushes, to photograph, and map a single body. But it is the attention to detail that will hopefully pay off in the form of a conviction of the perpetrators. Snow tells his crews, "Lose one tooth or even a foot bone, and you're an accomplice to the crime."

A Worldwide Effort

Dr. Snow's students in Argentina went on to form the Equipo Argentino de Antropología Forense or Argentinean Forensic Anthropology Team (EAAF), the first national organization of its kind. They have also gone on to help other countries exhume their mass graves and document their tragedies, like those in Guatemala, where 40 years of civil war left more than 150,000 dead and 45,000 still missing. Major exhumation projects have taken place in Bolivia, Brazil, El Salvador, Honduras, Ethiopia, Iraq, and Kurdistan. Guatemala, Chile, and the Philippines followed Argentina's lead and created national forensic anthropology teams as well. Soon to follow are Colombia, Costa Rica, Iraq, Kurdistan, Ethiopia, and Haiti.

There is no statute of limitations on murder or on human-rights violations. Thirty-four years after the Hungarian revolution of October 1956, a team of anthropologists worked to document the atrocities committed by the Soviet Army and identify the thousands of civilians and political prisoners dumped in unmarked mass graves.

Much of the forensic work is organized and funded by nongovernment organizations such as the American Association for the Advancement of Science, which supported Snow's work in Argentina, and Physicians for Human Rights, which has carried out excavations in more than 30 countries. Human Rights Watch organized a mission to Kurdistan after the 1991 Gulf War, and the Carter Center of Emory University supported a project in Ethiopia. The work carried out in Yugoslavia set a valuable precedent, as it was the first sanctioned and funded by the United Nations. A year after the international tribunal was convened to investigate crimes in the former Yugoslavia, a second tribunal was created to investigate the slaughter of civilians in Rwanda.

Within the short span of three months in 1994, Hutu extremists in Rwanda killed more than half a million Tutsi and moderate Hutus. In 1996, Haglund and dozens of other members of Physicians for Human

Rights worked in Rwanda to exhume 493 bodies, a fraction of those thought to have been killed in a single massacre in April 1995. To their horror they discovered that more than half of the victims were infants and children under 18 years of age. They had been killed by a blow to the head with a club or machete. Other victims were old men and women left to die where they fell.

One set of remains found lying on the side of the hill just beneath a church became known as Banana Man, because a banana tree was growing through his waist. At the time of his death, his left fibula near the ankle had been severed by a single machete blow, making it impossible for him to flee. His wrist was broken, and his hands were crisscrossed with deep cut marks, indicating he had his hands and arms up to protect himself. At some point, he must have given up and rolled over, receiving several wounds to his back, severing his shoulder blade in two places. A blow to his head fractured his skull. Although the violence in Rwanda had been the subject of nightly newscasts around the world, the stark reality of the slashed and shattered bones of an elderly man gave the criminal court irrefutable evidence.

Both missions to Yugoslavia and Rwanda supplied more than enough physical evidence to warrant the prosecution of top officials in both countries. Although many officials have been indicted for crimes against humanity, obtaining convictions has been a slow and expensive process. Trials are under way for many officials, including former Serb president Slobodan Milosevic, who has been charged with murder, torture, and the deportation of hundreds of thousands of civilians from Kosovo.

Perhaps more convictions will be made in the future, but until then, a push is on for the creation of a permanent international criminal tribunal. According to Justice Richard Goldstone, chief prosecutor of the UN War Crimes Tribunals, "If those who contemplate ethnic cleansing or other war crimes suspect that they may be investigated by an international criminal tribunal, if they suspect that investigators will dig up evidence of their crimes, there is at least a possibility that they may be dissuaded by their own self-interest from following that path."

16

BRINGING THEM HOME

HERE RESTS IN HONORED GLORY AN AMERICAN
SOLDIER KNOWN BUT TO GOD

—Inscription on the Tomb of the Unknown Soldier

Fifty-seven years after a U.S. Navy PV-1 Ventura bomber lifted off from its U.S. air base in the Aleutian Islands, its crew may finally be coming home. The plane disappeared on March 25, 1944, during a mission with four other planes to bomb targets on the Kurile Islands in northern Japan. Of the five planes that took off that day, only one successfully completed its mission. One plane crashed shortly after take-off, two others were forced to return to base because of extreme weather conditions, and one just disappeared.

It is that plane that a U.S. recovery crew found on the steep face of Mutnovskiy volcano on the Kamchatka peninsula in eastern Russia. Russian geologists apparently found the wreckage decades ago, but the discovery was never reported to the U.S. government until recently. In September 2001, a search-and-recovery team from the U.S. Army Central Identification Laboratory in Hawaii (CILHI) was sent to excavate the rubble for what remained of the seven crew members and bring them back to the United States for identification. The crew from the downed Ventura are only a fraction of the 78,000 soldiers still unaccounted for from battles that took place during World War II, but they will not be the last to come home.

Although the process of repatriating military remains is slow, it is continuous. Back in the 1840s, the U.S. government pledged to find all of its war dead and return them to American soil. Back then it meant bringing soldiers home from the Spanish-American War, and officials probably could not have foreseen that the United States would become involved in several wars halfway around the world. Even so, that pledge is honored more today than it was a hundred years ago.

The growth of the repatriation effort has paralleled the advancement of forensic anthropology, and some of the greatest names in the forensic field worked, at one time or another, for the government, repatriating lost servicemen—Thomas McKern, Mildred Trotter, T. Dale Stewart, Clyde Snow, William Maples, and dozens of others that have yet to make their mark in forensic work. As in the past, many of the techniques being developed today are used, tested, and perfected at the state-of-the-art CILHI facility housed at the Hickham Air Force Base in Hawaii.

Casualty Data

In order to repatriate human remains, they first have to be located. That work starts in the Casualty Data (CD) department of CILHI with CD analysts who sift through military records for possible locations of remains. They study casualty reports, search-and-rescue reports, line-of-duty investigations, and witness statements as well as conduct map searches. The CD analysts also maintain the personnel, medical, and dental files of all deceased servicemen and servicewomen who are still unaccounted for. This alone is a monumental task—some 2,100 military personnel are missing from Indochina, more than 8,100 from the Korean War, and more than 78,000 from World War II.

If the remains that come into the lab were recovered from a known crash site, then the records of those servicemen are pulled for further scrutiny. But sometimes, foreign governments return remains accompanied by little or no information regarding their geographic location or the details surrounding the discovery of the remains. In those instances, CD analysts pour through service members' files, looking for the best matching "loss scenario." Researchers will plot those individuals' last known locations on a map and carefully screen the accompanying service records.

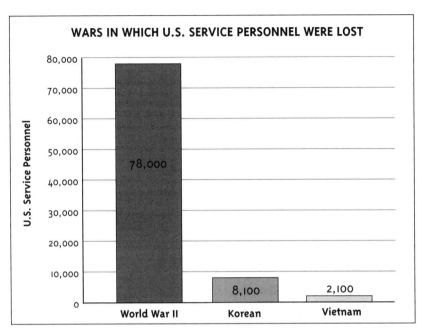

WARS IN WHICH U.S. SERVICE PERSONNEL WERE LOST

Unaccounted for military service personnel

Search and Recovery

CILHI maintains 14 search-and-recovery teams that are sent on missions several times a year. The crews are made up of military personnel, as well as civilian forensic anthropologists, and when needed may include linguists, medical specialists, or explosives experts. The teams go all over the world—to the slopes of Russian volcanoes, to the jungles of Cambodia, and rice fields of Vietnam—in search of human remains.

Those who are sent to Southeast Asia are overseen by Joint Task Force–Full Accounting, which was created in 1992 to specifically manage recoveries in that part of the world. The Joint Task Force includes more than 160 linguists, logistical experts, and forensic investigators who pinpoint the location of remains by scouring through war records and interviewing witnesses. Excavation sites are then located with the help of Global Positioning Systems, satellite images, and laser transits.

The Joint Task Force deploys six search-and-recovery teams to Vietnam approximately five times a year, three or four teams are sent to Laos four times a year, and two teams are deployed to Cambodia only once a year. The number of recovery missions carried out in North Korea is negotiated yearly, and there is one search-and-recovery team that devotes their time to excavating the remains of World War II service members and travels five times a year to various locations in Europe, Papua New Guinea, and China.

The missions are generally a month long and carry a full agenda. In October 2001, 95 specialists excavated six primary recovery sites and investigated another six "last known alive" scenarios throughout 12 Vietnamese provinces. In the past nine years, search-and-recovery crews have investigated more than 3,400 cases and conducted nearly 600 excavations, some of which centered around crash sites that stretched for miles. One plane that plowed straight through four mountain ridges left a potential excavation site that was nearly three miles long, all of which was carefully excavated for 25-year-old bone fragments.

A Mountaintop Mission

In the spring of 2001, Dave Rankin was the forensic anthropologist with a search-and-recovery crew sent to a cloud-covered mountain peak in Phou Louang in eastern Laos. It was the crash site of a U.S. Navy patrol plane, which flew its last mission in 1968. The plane was sent over the mountains to drop sensors into the jungle, allowing the U.S. Army to detect tremors from moving troops and eavesdrop on foreign military conversations. These sensors were also used by U.S. bombers to locate enemy convoys. But on January 11, 1968, the MR-2 Neptune and its crew of nine descended down into the clouds and never returned. Twelve days later the plane was found smashed 150 feet below the summit of the mountain. At the time, the near vertical slope and difficult terrain prevented a recovery crew from reaching them, but in 2001 Rankin and his men climbed up to a small ledge in an effort to locate all human remains.

Because of the steep angle of the mountain face, the recovery crew had to tether themselves with rope and climbing gear. Several team members shoveled soil from the small ledge and passed it to three others who poured the buckets out onto sifting screens, which hung from a tree limb. The sifters moved the soil carefully through the screening, examining anything bigger than a quarter of an inch. The soil crawled with leeches and foot-long centipedes, and poisonous vipers slid through the trees near the sifting screens. Rankin's team dug for six

A recovery crew from the U.S. Army Identification Lab excavates a site in Laos.
(Courtesy of Sergeant Shane J. Boucher of the United States Army Central Identification Laboratory, Hawaii [USA-CILHI])

days in thick heat and humidity without any sign of human remains, but on the seventh day they unearthed a thin curved piece of human skull—the first of many small fragments. After several accessible mountain ledges were excavated, the remains were taken back to CILHI for analysis. Like other military dead, the remains, which are kept in a wooden box, were placed in a coffin-sized aluminum case that was sealed and draped with the American flag and loaded onto the cargo plane by military personnel for the trip back to Hickham Air Force Base.

It is not certain that all nine crew members of the ill-fated Neptune will be identified, but their families have never given up hope. As Dave Rankin said in an interview, "Some of us do it for the families, to help them with closure. The ones I do it for, personally, are the guys. I do it for the guys up on the mountain."

The Identification Process

When a military soldier returns from a mission, he is given a proper welcome, and so, too, are his remains. As the cargo plane carrying the remains taxis into the airport at Hickham, a full honor guard is waiting. Representatives from all branches of the military in full-dress uniform solemnly carry the cases off the plane and into the morgue.

Inside CILHI, the remains are unsealed and removed. The lab employs 29 forensic anthropologists and four forensic odontologists who will analyze all bone fragments and dental material—a process that may take years. Each set of remains is first logged in, then taken to one of 20 examination tables that fill the large windowless room. The anthropologists first ask themselves, "Are all the bones human?" "How many people are represented by the assortment of bones?" It is common for remains that are turned over from a foreign government or by a refugee to include a few animal bones or be a commingling of several individuals.

Each set of human remains is then assigned to an anthropologist (not necessarily the same anthropologist who was present at the excavation) and an odontologist, if there are any dental remains. Both the anthropologist and odontologist work independently of each other to

Using archaeological techniques, a CILHI team excavates a World War II site in Makin Island. Note the sifting screens suspended from a pole behind the excavation. [Courtesy of Sergeant VeShanna J. Lovelace of the United States Army Central Identification Laboratory, Hawaii [USA-CILHI]]

Special equipment is used to recover remains from an underwater crash site off the coast of Makin Island. [Courtesy of Sergeant Chris Licking of the United States Army Central Identification Laboratory, Hawaii (USA-CILHI)]

ensure that their conclusions are not affected by the other's work. The reports of each scientist can then be cross-checked against the other.

Working with as many, or as few, bones as are available, the forensic anthropologist determines a biological profile—age, race, gender, stature, muscularity, antemortem anomalies and injuries, and perimortem trauma—for each individual. The forensic computer program, FORDISC 1.0 is used to determine the probability of whether a femur of a certain length comes from the same person as a tibia or other bone of a certain length. It also can help match bone fragments as well. Only when the biological profile is completed is it compared with known profiles of missing service members that are kept by the Casualty Data Department.

At the same time, a forensic odontologist works independently on any dentition that may be present. Full dental X rays are taken, and a dental profile of all restorations and identifying characteristics are documented. These findings are entered into a computer database called the Computer Assisted Post-Mortem Identification (CAPMI) system, which holds more than 2,500 dental records of U.S. service members who are unaccounted for. As many as 30 X rays of a single recovered tooth can be scanned into CAPMI, which searches its database, comparing dental profiles and generating a list of possible matches. The odontologist then pulls those files and compares the actual antemortem dental records and X rays with those taken of the remains. If the remains were recovered from a known crash site, then the search is narrowly focused on those crew members involved in the incident.

Although the forensic scientists work independently on one set of remains, they often receive help from scientists at the FBI, Armed Forces Institute of Pathology, Tripler Army Medical Center, and the Smithsonian Institution, as well as experts from their Visiting Scientist Program. When the biological and dental profiles are complete, the findings and all incident information such as maps, incident reports, search-and-recovery reports are brought to the scientific director, who will determine if the postmortem identifications, Casualty Data research, and other information is solid enough to be submitted for an independent review. No one anthropologist has the final say on the identification. It is a consensus. CILHI contracts with several board-certified experts to review all submitted identifications to either approve them or recommend more testing. All evidence must meet reasonable levels of scientific certainty before a positive identification is granted.

Sadly, there are remains that cannot be positively identified. It may be because the physical evidence was too fragmentary to determine a conclusive biological profile, or there was not enough casualty data to back up the physical evidence. In other situations, the antemortem evidence may not be adequate. For whatever reason, some remains end up stored away in an alcove for several years. But they are never forgotten. The anthropologists on staff at CILHI frequently take these bones off the shelf and study them again and again. It seems almost impossible to identify a person from no more than a single tooth or a handful of small bones, but it happens. Although the data banks may contain the files of thousands of healthy young men between the ages of 20 and 40 years old, they are well documented— a luxury that a forensic anthropologist working for a police department does not have—so it is possible that after many years, a soldier may be returned to his family.

It took 25 years before the family of 2nd Lieutenant Richard Vandegeer was finally able to bury his remains in Arlington National Cemetery in October 2000. Vandegeer's helicopter crashed in 1975 on Koh Tang Island in Cambodia, but it took 16 years and seven separate recovery missions—some on land and some in water—to recover the many commingled remains of what were believed to be 10 marine infantrymen and two navy corpsmen who were also aboard the helicopter at the time of the crash. The identification process that followed took nearly

10 more years. But as one serviceman said, "Any veteran would appreciate knowing that our country would care enough to come looking, remove us from a mudhole, and bring what was left back home." And each year more American soldiers come home. Since 1973, the remains of more than 630 American servicemen and servicewomen formerly unaccounted for have been identified and returned to their families.

DNA Testing

The majority of the identifications that are made at CILHI are based on dental remains and X-ray comparison, rather than DNA. They currently do not have the funding or the facilities to conduct the kind and quantity of DNA analysis required to identify all unaccounted for service members. Like fingerprints and dental identifications, DNA identification is also a comparative process and only works if there are samples of a service member's nuclear DNA or a sample of familial mtDNA to use for comparison. Prior to 1992, investigators did not have that kind of data on soldiers who fought in wars past.

Just after Desert Storm, in June of 1992, the Armed Forces Institute of Pathology created the first U.S. military DNA registry. Its files represent more than 1 million servicemen and servicewomen. Each person is represented by a small file card stained with two drops of blood smeared to the size of 50-cent pieces. These are housed in a freezer warehouse near Rockville, Maryland. Now that the groundwork has been laid with readily available DNA samples coupled with faster and more reliable testing methods, perhaps in the near future more identifications will be based on genetics. Until then, CILHI will continue to rely on the antemortem data that they currently have on file.

DNA analysis is often used to clear up disputes over remains. In 1998, a set of remains were taken out of the Tomb of the Unknowns at Arlington National Cemetery and tested. At the time that they were interred in 1984, scientists could not positively identify them. The remains were placed in the tomb in honor of all unaccounted for service members from the Vietnam War. Ten years later, however, additional evidence suggested that the remains might be 1st Lieutenant Michael Blassie, who died while flying an A-37 attack aircraft. He was shot down near An Loc in South Vietnam in 1972. The Blassie family petitioned to have the remains tested using mtDNA. The tests came back positive, and in July 1998 Blassie's remains were reburied near his family's home.

ELIGIBLE DONORS OF mtDNA SAMPLES

If you are related to an unaccounted for serviceman or servicewoman, you might be eligible to donate mtDNA for comparison testing. Eligible donors must be related on the person's maternal side. Those shown in gray are eligible to give a sample. Those in white are not.

Although the Tomb of the Unknowns still holds the unidentified remains of soldiers killed in World War I, World War II, and the Korean War, it no longer holds remains of a soldier from the Vietnam War. And because of the genetic technology available to forensic scientists today, that section of the tomb will most likely remain empty, and veterans groups believe that someday there will be no unidentified soldiers, even from past wars. But this goal can only be attained if there are familial DNA samples made available for comparison. To that end, CILHI encourages the families of all unaccounted for military personnel to get involved before it is too late. According to CILHI, the number of eligible blood donors (the source of mtDNA) is in decline, and these samples are vital to ensure future identifications. They are requesting that all maternal relatives of World War II, Korean War, cold war, and Vietnam War casualties contact the appropriate branch of the military and find out if they are suitable donors. Perhaps some of the crew members of the PV-1 Ventura discovered up on Mutnovskiy volcano in Russia may be identified with the help of a brother or sister, a niece or nephew, or even a second cousin they never knew.

After September 11

Not all victims of war are tallied by generals in the armed forces. On September 11, 2001, they were counted by CEOs of companies like Morgan Stanley Dean Witter, Cantor Fitzgerald, and Fiduciary Trust Company International, companies that once occupied offices in the World Trade Center.

The crime scene at the World Trade Center—16 acres wide and nine stories high—changed the face of forensic investigations forever. [FEMA]

The violence unleashed that day had never been seen in such magnitude before, and it changed forensic investigation forever. Never before had such devastation resulted in so many fragmented human remains. The sheer force of the disaster changed the way bodies had to be examined and identified. "The work of the forensic anthropologist will become more and more important," said Frank Saul, regional commander of Disaster Mortuary Operation Response Team V. "Because we are the ones who can take a small fragment and say this comes from the right arm, or this bit of tissue and bone comes from the back of the thigh." The forensic anthropologist can do what no other specialist can. "Given only fragments, we can recreate a biological profile of sex, age, ancestry, stature, and body use, and decipher if there is more than one individual represented."

In the future, forensic anthropologists will also play an enhanced role in recovery, as archaeological techniques become a mandated part of stricter search-and-recovery protocol not only at mass disaster sites but also at suspected homicide scenes. The use of specialized computer programs to collect antemortem data and determine statistics and biological profiles will also increase. As evidence becomes more fragmentary, anthropological research may shift to the microscopic level in order to glean the most information from the smallest bits of human remains.

As with all forensic sciences, forensic anthropology will evolve and keep pace with the criminals. Unfortunately, the workload of homicide victims, car crash fatalities, and mass disaster cases will never end. Just weeks after the first DMORT crews were sent home to rest from their tour of duty at the World Trade Center site, another disaster struck. On November 12, 2001, American Airlines Flight 587 crashed into a suburban community of Belle Harbor, Queens, killing 265 people. Forensic anthropologists were on hand to help recover and identify the human remains.

GLOSSARY

adipocere   A waxy white material that is formed when body fat decays in the presence of moisture.

antemortem   Before death.

anthropology   The study of humans, their cultures and societies.

anthropometry   The study of human body measurements.

articulated   Two adjacent bones joined together.

autolysis   The natural process of decomposition, where the enzymes in a corpse digest the body.

cancellous tissue   The spongy, porous interior of bone.

cortex   The hard, dense outer layer of bone.

cranial suture   The seam where two bones of the skull meet and fuse together.

cremains   The fragmentary remains of a body after cremation.

diaphysis   The shaft of the long bones.

DNA   Deoxyribonucleic acid; the genetic material inside every living cell that dictates its form and function.

epiphysis   The joint end of the long bones.

exhume   To dig out of a grave or tomb.

facial approximation   The process of forming a face based on the measurements and contours of the skull.

forensic   A legal argument or procedures that can be used in a court of law.

forensic entomology   The study of insects to help solve criminal cases.

forensic odontologists   Scientists who study how the teeth and dental work of dead individuals can establish their identity.

innominate   The hip bone; one side of the pelvis made up of three bones fused together.

instar   A stage in the growth of a maggot or insect larva.

long bones   The bones of the arms and legs; humerus, radius, ulna, femur, tibia, and fibula.

modeling   The changes that occur in the skeletal structure due to natural maturation from birth to adulthood.

mitochondrial DNA (mtDNA)   Deoxyribonucleic acid found in the mitochondria of a cell and passed down through the maternal line.

ossification   The natural process of the formation and hardening of the bones.

osteometric board   A tool for measuring the length of the long bones.

osteons   Circular tunnels within bone that hold blood vessels and nerve fibers.

PCR   Polymerase Chain Reaction; a process that duplicates small and degraded amounts of DNA.

perimortem   At or near the time of death.

phalanges   Finger and toe bones.

postmortem   After death.

postmortem interval   The amount of time that elapsed between the moment of death and discovery of the body.

pubic symphysis   The surface of the pubic bone where the two halves of the pelvis meet.

putrefaction   The natural process of decomposition, where bacteria in a dead body continue to reproduce and feed.

remodeling   The changes that occur in the skeletal structure of an adult due to nutritional deficiencies, disease, or injury.

repatriate   To return the remains of the dead to their homelands.

superimposition   A photographic technique that places a photo of a skull over a portrait of a person in order to compare skeletal and facial features.

taphonomy   The study of the changes that occur to a corpse after death.

FURTHER READING

Burns, Karen Ramey. *Forensic Anthropology Training Manual.* Upper Saddle River, N.J.: Prentice Hall, 1999.

Goff, M. Lee. *A Fly for the Prosecution: How Insect Evidence Helps Solve Crimes.* Cambridge, Mass.: Harvard University Press, 2000.

Goldstone, Richard J. *For Humanity: Reflections of a War Crimes Investigator.* New Haven, Conn.: Yale University Press, 2000.

Joyce, Christopher, and Eric Stover. *Witnesses from the Grave.* Boston, Mass.: Little, Brown and Co., 1991.

Larsen, Clark Spencer. *Skeletons in Our Closet: Revealing Our Past through Bioarchaeology.* Princeton, N.J.: Princeton University Press, 2000.

Manhein, Mary H. *The Bone Lady: Life as a Forensic Anthropologist.* New York: Penguin Books, 1999.

Maples, William, and Michael Browning. *Dead Men Do Tell Tales.* New York: Doubleday, 1994.

Nafte, Myriam. *Flesh and Bone: An Introduction to Forensic Anthropology.* Durham, N.C.: Carolina Academic Press, 2000.

Owen, David. *Hidden Evidence.* Willowdale, Ontario: Firefly Books, 2000.

Pringle, Heather. *The Mummy Congress: Science, Obsession and the Everlasting Dead.* New York: Theia Books, 2001.

Reichs, Kathleen J., ed. *Forensic Osteology: Advances in the Identification of Human Remains,* 2nd ed. Springfield, Ill.: Charles C. Thomas, 1998.

Rhine, Stanley. *Bone Voyage: A Journey in Forensic Anthropology.* Albuquerque, N.M.: University of New Mexico Press, 1998.

Stover, Eric, and Gilles Peress. *The Graves: Srebrenica and Vukovar.* Zurich, Switzerland: Scalo, 1998.

Ubelaker, Douglas, and Henry Scammell. *Bones.* New York: HarperCollins, 1992.

WEBSITES

American Academy of Forensic Sciences
http://www.aafs.org

American Board of Forensic Anthropology
http://www.csuchico.edu/anth/ABFA/

American Board of Forensic Entomology
http://www.missouri.edu/~agww/entomology

American Board of Forensic Odontology
http://www.abfo.org

C. A. Pound Human Identification Laboratory
http://web.anthro.ufl.edu/c.a.poundlab/poundlab.htm

The Crime Library
http://www.crimelibrary.com

The Federal Bureau of Investigation
http://www.fbi.gov

The University of Tennessee Forensic Anthropology Center
http://web.utk.edu/~anthrop/

U.S. Army Central Identification Laboratory Hawaii
http://www.cilhi.army.mil

INDEX

Italic page numbers indicate illustrations.